Moun·

A Daily Spiritual Journey for Hikers

A Daily Bible-based Devotional
Six-Month-One-Year Edition

From award winning author
Mark Stephen Taylor

To Michael
MAy your Journey THROUGH
THis Book Be one of Enlightenment

love pine cld
9/3/1

Mountain Meditations
A Daily Spiritual Journey for Hikers

A Daily Bible-based Devotional; Six-Month-One-Year Edition
(Hiking the Trail of Truth Volume VI) 7/20/17 edition

by *Mark Stephen Taylor*

Printed in the United States of America
ISBN-10: 1508627142
ISBN-13: 978-1508627142

Unless otherwise stated, Biblical quotations are taken from the following versions of the Bible:
(1) Thompson Chain-Reference, New American Standard Bible, Copyright © 1993, by, B. B. Kirk Bride Bible Company, Inc. In-text = (NASB)
(2) New Geneva Study Bible, New King James Version, Copyright © 1982, by Thomas Nelson Inc. In-text = (NKJV)
(3) The New International Bible, Copyright © 1983, by the International Bible Society. In-text = (NIV)

Italicized words in text are for emphasis.

The author designs any graphics in this book. Photos in

this book were taken by the author and remain the property of the author.

*Any portion of this book may be reproduced for teaching and classroom use. All information in this book is directly from the Bible. Any references used to enhance this information are super-scripted and indicated on the *References and Notes'* page, in the back of this book. Any statements found within this writing that are similar to other publications not mentioned are purely coincidental.

MSTaylor Productions, Lone Wolf Limited
hikemark@hotmail.com

3

From
LONE WOLF LIMITED

A Division Of
M S Taylor Productions
PO Box 547, Lone Pine, CA 93545
Phone: 909-549-0068

Dedication

In memory of
Pauline Evelyn Boley Taylor
1918-1959

MOUNTAIN MEDITATIONS
A Daily Spiritual Journey for Hikers;
A Daily Bible-based Devotional,
January thru June and July thru December Edition

FORWARD, from the author...

This particular book was designed especially for all hikers who have a love of the high country. The volume contains daily meditations, quite carefully selected from the Bible, and arranged in a manner so as to teach, enlighten, and bring inspiration along the high trails. This is indeed a perpetual volume, in that it never ceases to encourage. The words of God endure forever, and so new insights are gleaned each time that we read through them, time after time.

My personal wanderings into the high country were and continue to be my best times with God—alone or with others. It is there where I can so vividly encounter the wonders of His creation. My varied experiences and the grace of God have allowed me to indeed behold the supernatural through the natural amidst the high rocks, and among the vast, captivating desert landscapes as well.

The Scriptures that I have selected for this devotional are like a mere drop of water in a heavy downpour of rain. Yet, a single drop of water in a barren wasteland would be a find of great significance to one who is truly thirsty—one who yearns for meaningful and satisfying enlightenment. I hope that you will choose to carry this edition of 'Mountain Meditations' along with you in your day-pouch or backpack the very next time you hike the high trails—or any trails for that matter. It can open your eyes to many things, as you associate the wonders around you with the entirely spiritual, Biblical precepts that you are about to read, meditate upon, and gain insight from each day.

There is no human philosophy nor Biblical commentary associated with this volume. The Scriptures are the greatest treasure on earth, and in and of themselves serve to arouse the heart and stimulate one's thinking along the trail to maturity—nothing else is needed. They are the pot of gold at the end of the rainbow. Have a great journey!

Open my eyes, Lord, that I may see wondrous things from your law. (Psalm 119:18)

Sincerely, *Mark S Taylor*

January 1st / July 1st

Then God said, "Let there be light," and there was light...

¤ The heavens declare the glory of God, and their expanse declares the work of His hands. Day after day they speak, and night after night they instruct. There is no place in the universe where their voice is not heard. Their sound has gone out through all the earth, and their words to the end of the world.

In the heavens He has made an evening shelter for the sun, which rises in radiance like a bridegroom making his way to the wedding. It revels as a strong athlete, ready to run its race. Its rising is from one end of heaven, and its circuit to the other end. There is nothing hidden from its heat.

¤ There is one glory of the sun, another glory of the moon, and still another glory of the stars, for one star differs from another star in majesty and illumination.

¤ God is wise in heart and mighty in strength. Who has forgotten Him within their heart and prospered? He can remove mountains without warning, overturning them in His anger. He can shake the earth out of its place so that its very foundations tremble. He can command the sun and it will not rise. He can eclipse the sun or cause the stars not to be seen.

He alone spreads out the heavens and walks on the waves of

the sea. He made the Bear, Orion, and the Pleiades, and the constellations of the southern sky. He does great things, which we cannot comprehend; yes, wonders without number. If He goes by me, I do not see Him. If He moves past, I do not know that He is there. If He takes away, who can hinder Him? Who can say to Him, "What are You doing?"

¤ Can you search out the deep things of God? Can you find out the limits of the Almighty? They are higher than heaven... What can you do?

¤ Hear me... Believe in the Lord your God, and you shall be established. Believe His prophets, and you shall prosper. ¤ You shall be like a tree planted by streams of water, which yields its fruit in season. ¤ Your sun shall no longer go down, nor shall your moon withdraw itself; for the Lord will be your everlasting light, and the days of your grieving, yearning and aching shall all be ended.

Genesis 1:3, Psalm 19:1-7, 1st Corinthians 15:41, Job 9:4-12,
Job 11:7, 8, 2nd Chronicles 20:20, Psalm 1:3, Isaiah 60:20

9

January 2ⁿᵈ / July 2ⁿᵈ

I sustained you on eagles' wings and brought you to Myself...

Now therefore, if you will indeed obey My voice and keep My covenant, then you shall be a special treasure to Me above all people; for all the earth is Mine.
¤ In a desert wilderness I found you, in a barren and howling waste. I shielded you and cared for you and guarded you as the apple of My eye; like an eagle that stirs up its nest and hovers over its young ones and carries them on its wings.
¤ I have upheld you since you were born, and carried you along since your youth. Even to your old age and gray hairs I am He; I am He who will bare you up. I have made you and I will care for you; I will sustain you and I will come and rescue you. ¤ For this God is our God forever and ever; He will be our guide even to the end.
¤ Praise the Lord, O my soul, and forget not all His mercies

—Who forgives all your sins and heals all your diseases, Who redeems your life from the pit and crowns you with love and compassion, Who satisfies your desires with good things, so that your youth is renewed like the eagle's.

¤ Do you not know? Have you not heard? The Lord is the everlasting God, the Creator of the ends of the earth. He will not grow tired or weary, and His understanding no one can fathom. He gives power to the weak, and to those who have no might He increases in strength.

Even youths grow tired and weary, and young men stumble and utterly fall. But those who wait on the Lord shall renew their strength; they shall mount up with wings like eagles, they shall run and not be weary, they shall walk and not faint.

¤ He will not break the bruised reed, nor quench the dimly burning flame; He will encourage the fainthearted, those tempted to despair.

¤ Wait on the Lord. Be of good courage and He will strengthen your heart. Wait, I say, on the Lord!

Exodus 19:4, 5,
Deuteronomy 32:10, 11,
Isaiah 46:3, 4, Psalm 48:14,
Psalm 103:2-5, Isaiah 40:28-31,
Isaiah 42:3, Psalm 27:14

11

January 3rd / July 3rd

*So I say, live by the Spirit,
and you will not gratify the
desires of the sinful nature.*

For the sinful nature desires what is contrary to the Spirit, and the Spirit what is contrary to the sinful nature. They are in conflict with each other, so that you cannot do those things that you want to do. But if you are led by the Spirit, you are not under the law. The acts of the sinful nature are obvious: sexual immorality, impurity and eagerness for lustful pleasure, idolatry, participation in demonic activities, hostility, quarreling, jealousy, outbursts of anger, selfish ambition, divisions, factions, envy, drunkenness, wild parties and the like. I warn you, as I did before, that those who live like this will not inherit the kingdom of God.

But the fruit of the Spirit is love, joy, piece, patience, kindness, goodness, faithfulness, gentleness and self-control. Here there is no conflict with the law. Those who belong to Christ Jesus have crucified the sinful nature with its passions and desires. God's Spirit has given us life, and so we should follow the leading of the Spirit. Let us not become conceited, or irritate one another, or be jealous of one another.

¤ I pray... that you will begin to understand the incredible greatness of His power for us who believe in Him. This is the same mighty power that raised Christ from the dead and seated

Him in the place of honor at God's right hand in the heavenly realms. He is far above any ruler or authority or power or leader or anything else in this present world, or in the world to come.
¤ Follow God's example in everything you do, because you are His dear children. Live a life filled with love for others, following the example of Christ, who loved you and gave Himself as a sacrifice to take away your sins. And God was pleased, because that sacrifice was like sweet perfume to Him...

For though your hearts were once full of darkness, now you are full of light from the Lord, and your behavior should show it. For this light within you produces only what is good and right and true... So be careful how you live, not as fools but as those who are wise. Make the most of every opportunity for doing good in these evil days. Don't act thoughtlessly, but try to understand what the Lord wants you to do.

¤ I am sure that God, who began the good work within you, will continue His work until it is finally finished on that day when Christ Jesus comes back again.

¤ I say then: Walk in the Spirit.

Galatians 5:16-26, Ephesians 1:19-21,
Ephesians 5:1, 2, 8, 9, 15-17, Philippians 1:6,
Galatians 5:16

January 4th / July 4th

Does not wisdom cry out, and
understanding lift up her voice?

She[1] takes her stand on the top of the high hill, beside the way, where the paths meet. She cries out by the gates at the entrance to the city, at the very doors:

"To you, O men, I call, and my voice is to all people. O you naive ones, understand common sense, and you fools, be of an understanding heart. Listen, for I will speak of excellent things, and from the opening of my lips will come right things, for my mouth will speak truth.

"Wickedness is an abomination to my lips. All the words of my mouth are with righteousness; nothing crooked or perverse is in them. They are all plain to him who understands, and right to those who find knowledge. Receive my instruction and not silver, and knowledge rather than choice gold, for wisdom is better than rubies, and all the things one may desire cannot be compared with her.

"I wisdom, dwell with prudence, and possess knowledge and discretion. The fear of the Lord is to hate evil, pride and arrogance, evil behavior and perverse speech. Counsel is mine and sound wisdom. I am understanding, I have strength. By me kings and presidents reign, and rulers decree justice. By me princess rule, and nobles, all judges of the earth. I love those who love me, and those who seek me diligently will find me.

"Riches and honor are with me, enduring riches and righteousness. My fruit is better than gold, yes, than fine gold, and my revenue than choice silver. I traverse the way of righteousness, in the midst of the paths of justice, that I may

14

cause those who love me to inherit wealth, that I may fill their treasuries. "The Lord possessed me at the beginning of His way, before His works of old. I have been established from everlasting; from the beginning before there ever was an earth. When there were no oceans I was brought forth, when there were no fountains abounding with water. Before the mountains were settled in place, before the hills, I was brought forth, while as yet He had not made the earth or the outer places, or the primal dust of the world.

"When He prepared the heavens I was there, when He marked out the horizon on the face of the deep, when He established the clouds above, when He strengthened the fountains of the deep, when He assigned to the sea its limit, so that the waters would not transgress His command, when He marked out the foundations of the earth, then I was beside Him as His master craftsman, and I was filled with delight day after day, rejoicing always before Him; rejoicing in His inhabited world. And my delight was with the human race!

"Now then, my sons, listen to me; blessed are those who keep my ways. Listen to my instruction and be wise; do not ignore it. Blessed is the man who listens to me, watching daily at my doors, waiting at my doorway. For whoever finds me finds life and receives favor from the Lord. But whoever fails to find me harms himself, and all who hate me love death."

Proverbs, Chapter 8

January 5th / July 5th

O, Lord, You have examined my heart and know everything about me...

You know when I sit down or stand up. You know my every thought when far away. You chart the path ahead of me and tell me where to stop and rest. Every moment You know where I am. You know what I am going to say even before I say it, Lord. You both proceed and follow me. You place Your hand of blessing upon my head. Such knowledge is too wonderful for me, too great for me to know!

I can never escape from Your Spirit! I can never get away from Your presence! If I go up to heaven, You are there; if I go down to the place of the dead, You are there. If I ride the wings of the morning, if I dwell by the farthest oceans, even there Your hand will guide me, and Your strength will support me.

16

I could ask the darkness to hide me and the light around me to become night—but even in darkness I cannot hide from You. To You the night shines as bright as day. Darkness and light are both alike to You.

You made all the delicate, inner parts of my body and knit me together in my mother's womb. Thank You for making me so wonderfully complex! Your workmanship is marvelous—and how well I know it. You watched me as I was being formed in utter seclusion, as I was woven together in the dark of the womb. You saw me before I was born.

Every day of my life was recorded in Your book. Every moment was laid out before a single day had passed. How precious are Your thoughts about me, O God! They are innumerable! I can't even count them; they outnumber the grains of sand! And when I awaken in the morning, You are still with me!

¤ Bow down Your ear, O Lord. Hear me, answer me, for I need Your help. Preserve my life, for I am devoted to You; You are my God. Save Your servant who trusts in You! Be merciful to me, O Lord, for I cry to You all day long. Make glad the soul of Your servant, for to You, O Lord, I lift up my soul; my life depends on You.

For You, O Lord, are good, and ready to forgive. You are full of abundant mercy to all those who call upon You. Give ear, O Lord, to my prayer, and attend to the voice of my earnestness. In the day of my trouble I will call upon You, for I know You will answer me.

Psalm 139:1-18, Psalm 86:1-7

January 6th / July 6th

And the Lord said, "Stand on this glorious rock beside Me."

¤ After these things the word of the Lord came to Abraham in a vision, saying, "Do not be afraid, Abraham. I am your shield, your exceedingly great reward... Now, look toward the heavens and count the stars, if you are indeed able to number them. Your descendants will be like them; too many to count." And Abraham believed in the Lord, and the Lord declared him righteous because of his faith.

¤ Listen, O heavens, and I will speak. Hear, O earth, the words of My mouth. My teaching will fall on you like rain. My speech will settle like the dew. As raindrops on young plants, and as gentle showers on tender blades of grass, My words proclaim the name of the Lord. Ascribe greatness to our God. He is the Rock. His work is perfect. Everything He does is just and fair. He is a faithful God who does no wrong. How just and upright He is!

¤ The Lord is my rock, my fortress, and my deliverer. He is the God of my strength, in whom I will trust. He is my shield, the strength of my salvation, and my stronghold, my high tower, my Savior, the One who protects me from violence. I will call on the Lord, who is worthy to be praised, for He saves me from all my enemies...

They confronted me in the day of my calamity, but the Lord

18

was my support. He brought me out into a place of safety. He rescued me because He delights in me. The Lord rewarded me for doing right, because of my innocence in His sight. For I have kept the ways of the Lord, and have not wickedly departed from His teachings, for His statutes are written upon my heart.

    ¤ For you are all sons of God through faith in Christ Jesus. For as many of you as were baptized into Christ, have put on Christ. There is neither Jew nor Greek, there is neither slave nor free, there is neither male nor female; for you are all one in Christ Jesus. And if you are Christ's, then you are Abraham's seed, and heirs according to the promise.

    ¤ For the promise that Abraham would be heir of the world was not made to him or his seed through the law, but through a relationship with God that comes by faith.

    ¤ Moreover, brethren, I do not want you to be unaware that all our fathers were under the cloud, all passed through the sea, all were baptized into Moses in the cloud and in the sea, all ate the same spiritual food, and all drank the same spiritual drink. For they drank of that spiritual Rock that followed them, and that Rock was Christ.

Exodus 33:21, Genesis 15:1, 5, 6, Deuteronomy 32:1-4,
2nd Samuel 22:1-4, 19-23, Galatians 3:26-29, Romans 4:13,
1ˢᵗ Corinthians 10:1-4

January 7th / July 7th

 The lamp of the body is the eye. Therefore, when your eye is sound, your whole body is full of light. But if your eye is evil, your whole body will be full of darkness.

Be very careful then that the light within you never becomes darkness. If your body is full of light, having no part dark, the whole body then will be radiant—it will be like a bright lamp giving off its light!

¤ Trust in the Lord and do good. Dwell in the land and feed on His faithfulness. Delight yourself also in the Lord, and He shall give you the desires of your heart. Commit your way to the Lord. Trust also in Him and He will help you. He shall bring forth your redemption as the light, and the justice of your cause as the noonday sun.

¤ The Lord is my light and my salvation; Whom shall I fear? ¤ In Galilee of the Gentiles, the people who walked in darkness have seen a great light; Those who dwelt in the land of the shadow of death, upon them a light has dawned. ¤ Jesus said, "I am the light of the world. He who follows Me shall not walk in darkness, but have the light of life." ¤ Come and let us walk in the light of the Lord.

¤ God is light and in Him there is no darkness at all. If we say that we have fellowship with Him, and walk in darkness, we lie and do not practice the truth. But if we walk in the light as He is in the light, we have fellowship with one another, and the blood of Jesus Christ His Son cleanses us from all sin.

20

If we say that we have no sin, we only deceive ourselves, and the truth is not in us. If we confess our sins, He is faithful and just to forgive us our sins, and to cleanse us from all unrighteousness.

¤ The sun shall no longer be your light by day, nor for brightness shall the moon give light to you; But the Lord will be to you an everlasting light, and your God your glory. Your sun shall no longer go down, nor shall your moon withdraw itself; For the Lord will be your everlasting light, and the days of your mourning shall be ended.

¤ For it is God who commanded light to shine out of darkness, and He has made us to understand that this light is the brightness of the glory of God that is seen in the face of Jesus Christ.

¤ You are the light of the world; a city that is set on a hill cannot be hidden. Nor do people light a lamp and put it under a basket, but on a lamp stand, and it gives light to all who are in the house. Let your light so shine before men, that they may see your good works and glorify your Father in heaven.

Luke 11:34-36, Psalm 37:3-6, Psalm 27:1, Isaiah 9:1, 2,
John 8:12, Isaiah 2:5, 1st John 1:5-9, Isaiah 60:19, 20,
2nd Corinthians 4:6, Matthew 5:14-16

21

January 8th / July 8th

Lift up a banner on the high mountains.
Raise your voice to them.

¤ Lord, You have been our dwelling place in all generations. Before the mountains were brought forth, or ever You had formed the earth and the world, even from everlasting to everlasting, You are God.

¤ Those who trust in the Lord are like Mount Zion, which cannot be moved, but abides forever. As the mountains surround Jerusalem, so the Lord surrounds His people. From this time forth and forever.

¤ Sing to the Lord with thanksgiving; Sing praises on the harp to our God, Who covers the heavens with clouds, Who prepares the rain for the earth, Who makes grass to grow on the mountains. He gives to the beast its food, and to the young ravens that cry. He does not delight in the strength of the horse; He takes no pleasure in the legs of a man. The Lord takes pleasure in those who fear Him, in those who hope in His mercy.

¤ Praise the Lord from the earth, you great sea creatures and all the depths; Fire and hail, snow and clouds; Stormy wind, fulfilling His word; Mountains and all hills; Fruitful trees and all cedars; Beasts and all cattle; Creeping things and flying fowl; Kings of the earth and all peoples; Princes and all judges of the earth; Both young men and maidens; Old men and children.

Let them praise the name of the Lord, for His name alone is exalted; His glory is above the earth and heaven.

Isaiah 13:2, Psalm 90:1, 2, Psalm 125:1, 2, Psalm 147:7-11,
Psalm 149:7-13

January 9th / July 9th

Watch and pray lest you enter into temptation. The spirit indeed is willing, but the flesh is weak.

¤ I wait for the Lord, my soul waits, and in His word I do hope. My soul waits for the Lord, more then sentinels who long for the dawn, yes, more than watchmen who wait for the morning. ¤ I know that nothing good lives in me, that is, in my sinful nature. For I have the desire to do what is good, but I cannot carry it out. For what I actually do is not the good that I want to do; no, the evil that I do *not* want to do—this is what I keep on doing.

Now if I do what I do not want to do, it is no longer I who do it, but it is sin living in me that does it. So, I find this law at work: When I want to do good, evil is right there with me. For in my inner being I delight in God's law; but I see another law at work in the members of my body, waging war against the law of my mind and making me a prisoner of the law of sin at work in my members.

What a wretched man I am! Who will rescue me from this body of death? Thanks be to God—through Jesus Christ our Lord! So then, I myself in my mind am a slave to God's law, but in my sinful nature I am a slave to the law of sin. ¤ For Your namesake, O Lord, pardon my iniquity, for it is great!

¤ You are all sons of God through faith in Christ Jesus, for all of you who were baptized into Christ have clothed yourself with Christ.

Matthew 26:41, Psalm 130:5, 6, Romans 7:18-25, Psalm 25:11, Galatians 3:26, 27

24

January 10th
July 10th

"Come now, and let us reason together," says the Lord.

"Though your sins are like scarlet, they shall be as white as snow; though they are red like crimson, they shall be as wool. If you are willing and obedient, you shall eat the good of the land." ¤ For as high as the heavens are above the earth...As far as the east is from the west, so far has He removed our transgressions from us.

¤ Now it shall come to pass in the latter days that the mountain of the Lord's house shall be established on the top of the mountains, and shall be exalted above the hills; And all nations shall flow into it. Many people shall come and say, "Come and let us go up to the mountain of the Lord, to the house of the God of Jacob; He will teach us His ways, and we shall walk in His paths."

¤ I tell you the truth, no one can enter the kingdom of God unless he is born of water and the Spirit. ¤ ...They ate their food with gladness and simplicity of heart, praising God and having favor with all the people. And the Lord added to the church daily those who were being saved.

Isaiah 1:18,19, Psalm 103:11,12, Isaiah 2:1-3, John 3:5, Acts 2:46,47

January 11th / July 11th

Be very careful then how you live—not as unwise but as wise, making the most of every opportunity, because the days are evil.

¤ He has shown you, O man, what is good; And what does the Lord require of you? To act justly and to love mercy and to walk humbly with your God.

¤ The God who made the world and everything in it is the Lord of heaven and earth, and does not live in temples built by hands. And He is not served by human hands, as if He needed anything, because He Himself gives all men life and breath and everything else. From one man He made every nation of men, that they should inhabit the whole earth; and He determined the times set for them and the exact places where they should live.

God did this so men would seek Him and perhaps reach out for Him and find Him, though He is not far from each one of us. For in Him we live and move and have our being... Therefore since we are God's offspring, we should not think that the Divine Being is like gold or silver or stone—an image made by man's design and skill. In the past God overlooked such ignorance, but now He commands all people everywhere to repent.

For He has set a day when He will judge the world with justice by the man He has appointed. He has given proof of this to all men by raising Him from the dead.

Ephesians 5:15, Micah 6:8, Acts 17:24-31

January 12ᵗʰ / July 12ᵗʰ

He who forms the mountains, creates the wind, and reveals His thoughts to man; He who turns dawn to darkness, and treads the high places of the earth—the Lord Almighty is His name.

¤ If I have the gift of prophecy and can fathom all mysteries and all knowledge, and if I have a faith that can move mountains, but have not love, I am nothing... Love is patient, love is kind. It does not envy, it does not boast, it is not proud. It is not rude, it is not self-seeking, it is not easily angered, it keeps no record of wrongs. Love does not delight in evil but rejoices with the truth. It always protects, always trusts, always hopes, always perseveres. Love never fails.
¤ Beloved, let us love one another, for love is from God, and everyone who loves is born of God and knows God. ¤ And we know that all things work together for good to those who love God; for those who are the called according to His great purpose.

Amos 4:13, 1ˢᵗ Corinthians 13:2, 4-8, 1ˢᵗ John 4:7, Romans 8:28

January 13th / July 13th

The Lord Himself goes before you and will be with you; He will never leave you nor forsake you. Do not be afraid; do not be discouraged.

¤ I know, O Lord, that a man's life is not his own; it is not for man to direct his steps. Correct me, Lord, but only with justice—not in Your anger, lest You reduce me to nothing. ¤...I sinned, and perverted what was right, but I did not get what I deserved. He redeemed my soul from going down to the pit, and I will live to enjoy the light.

¤ The Lord redeems the soul of His servants, and none of those who trust in Him shall be condemned. ¤ Trust in the Lord with all your heart, and lean not on your own understanding; in all your ways acknowledge Him, and He shall direct your paths.

¤ "Let not the wise man boast in his wisdom, or the strong man boast in his strength, or the rich man boast of his riches, but let him who boasts boast about this: that he understands and knows Me, that I am the Lord, who exercises kindness, justice, and righteousness upon the earth, for in these I delight," declares the Lord.

¤ The Lord is my rock and my fortress and my deliverer, The God of my strength, in whom I will trust; My shield and the horn of my salvation; My stronghold and my refuge. ¤ I have gone astray like a lost sheep; seek Your servant, for I do not forget Your commandments.

Deuteronomy 31:8, Jeremiah 10:23, 24, Job 33:27, 28, Psalm 34:22, Proverbs 3:5,6, Jeremiah 9:23, 24, 2nd Samuel 22:2,3, Psalm 119:176

January 14th / July 14th

He sent from above, He took me, He drew me out of many waters. He delivered me... He delivered me because He delighted in me.

¤ The Lord is my shepherd, I shall not be in want. He makes me lie down in green pastures, He leads me beside quiet waters, He restores my soul. He guides me in the path of righteousness for His name's sake. Even though I walk through the valley of the shadow of death, I will fear no evil, for You are with me; Your rod and Your staff they comfort me.

¤ You, Lord, through Your commandments, make me wiser than my enemies; For they are ever with me. I have more understanding than all my teachers, for Your testimonies are my meditation. I understand more than the ancients, because I keep Your precepts.

2ⁿᵈSamuel 22:17, 18, 20, Psalm 23:1-4, Psalm 119:98-100

29

January 15th / July 15th

Ask the former generations and find out
what their fathers learned.

For we were born only yesterday and know nothing, and our days on earth are but a shadow. Will they not instruct you and tell you? Will they not bring forth words from their understanding?

Can papyrus grow tall where there is no marsh? Can reeds thrive without water? While still growing and uncut, they wither more quickly than grass. Such is the destiny of all who forget God; so perishes the hope of the godless. What he trusts in is fragile; what he relies on is a spider's web. He leans on the web, but it gives way; he clings to it, but it does not hold.

¤ Jesus said, "I am the way and the truth and the life. No one comes to the Father except through Me."

¤ The night is nearly over, the day is almost here. So let us put aside the deeds of darkness and put on the armor of light. Let us behave decently, as in the daytime, not in orgies or drunkenness, not in sexual immorality and debauchery, not in dissension and jealousy. Rather clothe yourselves with the Lord Jesus Christ, and do not think about how to gratify the desires of the sinful nature.

¤ Salvation is found in no one else, for there is no other name under heaven given among men by which we must be saved. ¤...As you have heard from the beginning, His command is that you walk in love.

Job 8:8-15, John 14:6, Romans13:12-14, Acts 4:12, 2nd John 1:6

January 16ᵗʰ / July 16ᵗʰ

On a high and lofty mountain I have set my bed; It was there I went up to offer sacrifices.

¤ The sacrifices of God are a broken spirit, a broken and contrite heart—these, O God, You will not despise.
¤ The Lord is good to those who wait for Him, to the soul who seeks Him. It is good that one should hope and wait quietly for the salvation of the Lord. It is good for a man to bear the yoke of discipline in his youth. Let him sit alone and keep silent, because God has laid it upon him; Let him bury his face in the dust—there may yet be hope.
¤ The fear of the Lord teaches a man wisdom, and humility comes before honor. ¤ Before his downfall a man's heart is proud, but humility comes before honor.
¤ By humility and the fear of the Lord are riches and honor and life. ¤ For whoever exalts himself will be humbled, but he who humbles himself will be exalted.

Isaiah 57:7, Psalm 51:17, Lamentations 3:25-29, Proverbs 15:33, Proverbs 18;12, Proverbs 22:4, Luke 14:11

31

January 17th / July 17th

If You, Lord, kept a record of sins, O Lord, who could stand? But with You there is forgiveness.

¤ Set a guard over my mouth, O Lord; keep watch over the door of my lips. Let not my heart be drawn to what is evil, to take part in wicked deeds.

¤ By wisdom the Lord laid the earth's foundations, by understanding He set the heavens in place; by His knowledge the deeps were divided, and the clouds let drop the dew. My son, preserve sound judgment and discernment, do not let them out of your sight; they will be life for you, and an ornament to grace your neck.

Then you will go on your way in safety, and your foot will not stumble; when you lie down, you will not be afraid; when you lie down your sleep will be sweet. Have no fear of sudden disaster, nor of the ruin that overtakes the wicked, for the Lord will be your confidence and will keep your foot from being snared.

¤ Get wisdom, get understanding; do not forget My words or swerve from them. Do not forsake wisdom, and she will protect you; love her and she will watch over you. Wisdom is supreme; therefore get wisdom. Though it cost all you have, get understanding. Esteem her, and she will exalt you; embrace her, and she will honor you. She will set a garland of grace on your head and present you with a crown of splendor.

Psalm 130:3, Psalm 141:3, 4, Proverbs 3:19-26, Proverbs 4:5-9

January 18ᵗʰ / July 18ᵗʰ

Jesus said to the blind man, "What do you want Me to do for you?" The man then replied, "Lord, I want to see."

¤ Open my eyes, that I might see wondrous things from Your law. I am a stranger on the earth, do not hide Your commands from me.

¤ Jesus said, "For judgment I have come into this world, so that the blind will see and those who see will become blind." Some Pharisees who were with Him heard Him say this and asked, "What? Are we blind too?"

Jesus then said, "If you were blind, you would not be guilty of sin; but now that you claim you can see, your guilt remains."

¤ "Woe to you, teachers of the law and Pharisees, you hypocrites! You shut up the kingdom of heaven against men; for you neither go in yourselves, nor do you allow those who are entering to go in."

¤ For to be carnally minded is death, but to be spiritually minded is life and peace. Because the carnal mind is enmity against God; for it is not subject to the law of God, nor indeed can be. So then, those who are in the flesh cannot please God. But you are not in the flesh but in the Spirit, if indeed the Spirit of God dwells in you. Now if anyone does not have the Spirit of Christ, he is not His.

¤ ...and He gave sight to many who were blind.

Luke 18:40, 41, Psalm 119:18, 19, John 9:39-41, Matthew 23:13, Romans 7:6-9, Luke 7:21

January 19th / July 19th

*The steps of a good man
are ordered by the Lord,
and He delights in his
way.*

Though he falls, he shall not be utterly cast down; for the Lord upholds him with His hand. I have been young and now I am old; yet, I have not seen the righteous forsaken, nor his descendants begging for bread. A righteous person is at all times merciful, and lends, and his descendants are blessed.

¤ Keep your lives free from the love of money and be content with what you have, because God has said, "Never will I leave you; never will I forsake you." So we can say with confidence, "The Lord is my helper; I will not be afraid. What can mere man do to me?"

¤ The Lord is righteous in all His ways and loving toward all that He has made. The Lord is near to all who call on Him, to all who call on Him in truth. He fulfills the desires of those who fear Him; He hears their cry and saves them. The Lord watches over all who love Him, but all the wicked He will destroy.

¤ For even the Son of Man did not come to be served, but to serve, and to give His life as a ransom for many. ¤ Do not be afraid...I am your shield, your very great reward.

*Psalm 37:23-26, Hebrews 13:5, 6, Psalm 145:17-20, Mark 10:45,
Genesis 15:1*

January 20th
July 20th

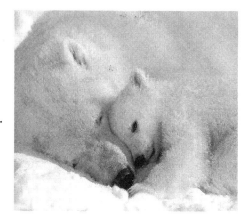

As the deer pants for streams of water, so my soul pants for you, O God.

My soul thirsts for God, for the living God. My tears have been my food day and night, while men say to me all day long, "Where is your God?"

¤ Show me Your ways, O Lord, teach me Your paths; guide me in Your truth and teach me, for You are God my Savior, and my hope is in You all day long. Remember, O Lord, Your great mercy and love, for they are from of old. Remember not the sins of my youth and my rebellious ways; according to Your love remember me, for You are good, O Lord... For the sake of Your name, O Lord, forgive my iniquity, though it is great.

¤ Here is a trustworthy saying that deserves full acceptance: Christ Jesus came into the world to save sinners—of whom I am the worst. But for that very reason I was shown mercy, so that in me, the worst of sinners, Christ Jesus might display His unlimited patience as an example for those who would believe on Him and receive eternal life.

Psalm 42:1-3, Psalm 25:4-7, 11, 1st Timothy 1:15, 16

35

January 21st / July 21st

But God remembered Noah...

And God remembered all the wild animals and livestock that were with him in the ark,[2] and He sent a wind over the earth, and the waters receded... And the waters decreased continually until the tenth month. In the tenth month, on the first day of the month, the tops of the mountains were seen. So it came to pass, at the end of forty days, that Noah opened the window of the ark which he had made. Then he sent out a raven, which kept going to and fro until the waters had dried up from the earth.

¤ The voice of the Lord strikes with flashes of lightning. The voice of the Lord shakes the wilderness...And in His temple everyone cries, "Glory!" The Lord sat enthroned at the Flood, and the Lord sits as King forever.

¤...God waited patiently in the days of Noah during the construction of the ark, in which a few, that is eight persons, were saved through water. Corresponding to that, baptism now saves you—not the removal of the filth of the flesh (the sinful nature), but an appeal to God for a good conscience—through the resurrection of Jesus Christ, who has gone to heaven and is at the right hand of God, angels and authorities and powers having been made subject to Him.

¤ And God said, "Whenever I bring clouds over the earth and the rainbow appears in the clouds, I will remember My covenant between Me and you and all living creatures of every kind. Never again will the waters become a flood to destroy all life...Whenever the rainbow appears in the clouds...this is the sign of the covenant."

Genesis 8:1, 5-7, Psalm 29:7-10, 1ˢᵗ Peter 3:20-22, Genesis 9:14-17

January 22nd / July 22nd

Oh, that You would rend the heavens and come down, that the mountains would tremble before You!

¤ Part your heavens, O Lord, and come down; touch the mountains, so that they smoke. Send forth lightning and scatter the enemies... ¤ We know that the whole creation has been groaning as in the pains of childbirth right up to the present time. Not only so, but we ourselves, who have the first-fruits of the Spirit, groan inwardly as we wait eagerly for our adoption as sons/daughters; the redemption of our bodies. For in this hope we were saved. But hope that is seen is not hope at all. Who hopes for what he already has? But if we hope for what we do not yet have, we wait for it patiently.

¤ Listen, I tell you a mystery... we will all be changed—in a flash, in the twinkling of an eye... the dead will be raised imperishable, and we will be changed. For the perishable must clothe itself with the imperishable, and the mortal with immortality... Death will be swallowed up in victory.

Isaiah 64:1, Psalm 144:5,6, Romans 8:22-25, 1st Corinthians 15:51-54

38

January 23rd / July 23rd

What I tell you in the darkness, speak in the light...

What you hear whispered in your ear, proclaim from the housetops. Do not fear those who kill the body but are unable to kill the soul; but rather fear Him who is able to destroy both soul and body in hell.

Are not two sparrows sold for a penny? Yet not one of them will fall to the ground apart from the will of your Father. And even the very hairs of your head are all numbered. So do not fear; you are more valuable than many sparrows.

¤ Go into all the world and preach the gospel to all creation. He who has believed and has been baptized will be saved; but he who has disbelieved shall be condemned.

¤ Every kingdom divided against itself will come to ruin, and every city or household divided against itself will not stand. If Satan drives out Satan, he is divided against himself. How then can his kingdom stand? ...But if I drive out demons by the Spirit of God, then the kingdom of God has come upon you.

¤ The work of God is this: to believe in the One He has sent.

Matthew 10:27-31, Mark 16:16, Matthew 12:25-28, John 6:29

January 24th / July 24th

*I am laid low in the dust;
preserve my life according
to Your word.*

I recounted my ways and You answered me; teach me Your decrees. Let me understand the teaching of Your precepts; then I will meditate on Your wonders.

My soul is weary with sorrow; strengthen me according to Your word. Keep me from deceitful ways; be gracious to me through Your law. I have chosen the way of truth; I have set my heart on Your laws. I hold fast to Your statutes, O Lord; do not let me be put to shame. I run in the path of Your commands, for You have set my heart free.

¤ Since you have been raised with Christ, set your hearts on things above, where Christ is seated at the right hand of God. Set your mind on things above, not on earthly things. ¤ Do nothing out of selfish ambition or vain conceit, but in humility consider others better than yourselves. Each of you should look not to your own interests, but also to the interests of others.

¤ Therefore, each of you must put off falsehood and speak truthfully to his neighbor, for we are all members of one body. ¤ Keep on loving each other as brothers. Do not forget to entertain strangers, for by so doing some people have entertained angels without knowing it. Remember those in prison as if you were their fellow prisoners, and those who are mistreated as if you yourselves were suffering.

*Psalm 119:25-32, Colossians 3:1, 2, Philippians 2:3, 4,
Ephesians 4:25, Hebrews 13:1-3*

January 25th / July 25th

*We can see and understand
only a little about God now,
as if we were peering at His
reflection in a poor mirror...*

But, someone we shall see
Him face to face. ¤ We did not
follow cleverly invented stories
when we told you about the
power and coming of our Lord
Jesus Christ, but were eyewitnesses to His majesty... And we
have the word of the prophets made more certain, and you will
do well to pay attention to it, as to a light shining in a dark
place, until the day dawns and the morning star rises in your
hearts.

Above all you must understand that no prophecy of
Scripture came about by the prophets own interpretation. For
prophecy never had its origin in the will of man, but men spoke
from God as they were carried along by the Holy Spirit. ¤ All
Scripture is God-breathed and is useful for teaching, rebuking,
correcting and training in righteousness, so that the man of God
may be thoroughly equipped for every good work.

¤ Dear children, this world's last hour has come... ¤ The
night is nearly over; the day is almost here. So put aside the
deeds of darkness and put on the armor of light. ¤ Let us
continue to encourage one another.

*1st Corinthians:13:12, 2nd Peter 1:16, 19-21, 2nd Timothy 3:16, 17,
1st John 2:18, Romans13:12, Hebrews 10:25*

41

January 26th / July 26th

*I will sing for the One I love a song
about His vineyard:*

My loved One had a vineyard on a fertile hillside. He dug it up and cleared it of stones and planted it with the choicest vines. He built a watchtower in it and cut out a wine press as well. And so, He expected it to bring forth good, sweet grapes—but it produced wild and sour grapes.

¤ "I had planted you like a choice vine of sound and reliable stock. How then did you turn against Me into a corrupt, wild vine? Although you wash yourself with lye and use an abundance of soap, the stain of your guilt is still before Me," declares the Sovereign Lord.

¤ When I kept silent, my bones wasted away through my groaning all day long. For day and night Your hand was heavy upon me; my strength was sapped as in the heat of summer. Then I acknowledged my sin to You and did not cover up my iniquity. I said, "I will confess my transgressions to the Lord"—and You forgave the guilt of my sin. Therefore let everyone who is godly pray to You while You may be found.

"I will instruct you and teach you in the way you should go," says the Lord. "I will counsel you and watch over you. Do not be like the horse or the mule which have no understanding, but must be controlled by a bit and bridle or they will not come to you." ¤ Everyone who calls on the name of the Lord will be saved. ¤ New wine will drip from the mountains and flow from all the hills.

*Isaiah 5:1, 2, Jeremiah 2:21, 22, Psalm 32:3-6, 8, 9, Joel 2:32,
Amos 9:13*

January 27th / July 27th

Do not despise the chastening of the Lord, nor detest His correction; For whom the Lord loves He corrects.

¤ Now no chastening seems to be joyful for the present, but painful; nevertheless, afterward it yields the peaceable fruit of righteousness to those who have been trained by it. Therefore strengthen the hands which hang down, and the feeble knees, and make straight paths for your feet, so that what is lame may not be disabled, but rather healed.

¤ So I say, live by the Spirit, and you will not gratify the desires of the sinful nature. ¤ Therefore we do not lose heart. Though outwardly we are wasting away, yet inwardly we are being renewed day by day. For our light and momentary troubles are achieving for us an eternal glory that far outweighs them all. So we fix our eyes not on what is seen, but on what is unseen. For what is seen is temporary, but what is unseen is eternal.

¤ During the days of Jesus' life on earth, He offered up prayers and petitions with loud cries and tears to the One who could save Him from death, and He was heard because of His reverent submission. Although He was a Son, yet He learned obedience from what He suffered, and being made perfect, He became the author of eternal salvation to all who obey Him.

¤ Consider it pure joy whenever you face trials of many kinds, because you know that the testing of your faith develops perseverance...maturity and completeness.

Proverbs 3:11, 12, Hebrews 12:11, 12, Galatians 5:16, 2nd Corinthians 4:16-18, Hebrews 5:7-9, James 1:2-4

January 28th / July 28th

*Let us run with patience the particular race that
God has set before us.*

Keep your eyes fixed on Jesus, the author and perfecter of our faith... ¤ Then Jesus said to them all, "If anyone would come after Me, he must deny himself and take up his cross daily and follow Me. For whoever wants to save his life will lose it, but whoever loses his life for My sake will save it.

"What good is it for a man to gain the whole world, and yet lose or forfeit his very self? If anyone is ashamed of Me and My words, the Son of Man will be ashamed of him when He comes in His glory, and in the glory of the Father and of the holy angels." ¤ The night is nearly over; the day is almost here. So let us put aside the deeds of darkness and put on the armor of light.

¤ Do you not know that in a race all the runners run, but only one of them gets the prize? Run in such a way as to get the prize. Everyone who competes in the games goes into strict training. They do it to get a crown that will not last; but we do it to get a crown that will last forever. Therefore, do not run like a man running aimlessly; do not fight like a man beating the air. No—instead buffet your body daily and bring it into subjection, so that you will not be disqualified for the prize.

¤ I press on toward the goal to win the prize for which God has called me heavenward in Christ Jesus. All of us who are mature should take such a view of things. And if on some point you think differently, that too God will make clear to you. Let us live up to what we've already attained. ¤ Let us acknowledge the Lord; let us press on to acknowledge Him. As surely as the sun rises, He will appear...

*Hebrews 12:1, 2, Luke 9:23-26, Romans 13:12,
1st Corinthians 9:24-27, Philippians 3:14-16, Hosea 6:3*

January 29th / July 29th

If one man sins against another, God will judge him. But if a man sins against the Lord, who will intercede for him?

¤ If anybody does sin, we have One who speaks to the Father in our defense—Jesus Christ, the righteous One. He is the atoning sacrifice for our sins, and not only for ours, but also for the sins of the whole world. ¤ If we claim we have not sinned, we make Him a liar and His word has no place in our lives. ¤ For all have sinned and fall short of the glory of God.

¤ What then shall we say in response to this? If God is for us, who can be against us? He who did not spare His own Son, but gave Him up for us all—how will He not also, along with Him, graciously give us all things? Who will bring any charge against those whom God has chosen?

¤ You are all sons of God through faith in Christ Jesus, for all of you who were baptized into Christ have clothed yourselves with Christ. There is neither Jew nor Greek, slave nor free, male nor female; for you are all one in Christ Jesus.

1st John 2:1, 2, 1st John 1:10, Romans 3:23, Romans 8:31-33, Galatians 3:26-29

January 30th / July 30th

The sun has one kind of splendor, the moon another and the stars another; and star differs from star in splendor.

¤ They had been arguing about which one of them was the greatest, and so Jesus called the twelve together and said to them, "If anyone wants to be first, he must be the very last, and the servant of all. ¤ You know that those who are regarded as rulers of the people lord it over them, and their high officials in turn exercise authority of them. Not so with you. Instead, whoever wants to become great among you must be your servant, and whoever wants to be first must be the slave of all. For even the Son of Man did not come to be served, but to serve, and to give His life as a ransom for many."

¤ Submit yourselves for the Lord's sake to every human institution, whether to a king as the one in authority, or to governors as sent by him for the punishment of evildoers and the praise of those who do right. For such is the will of God that by doing right you may silence the ignorance of foolish men.

1st Corinthians 15:41, Mark 9:33-35, Mark 10:42-45, 1st Peter 2:13-15

January 31st / July 31st

A certain ruler asked Jesus, "Good teacher, what must I do to inherit eternal life?"

"Why do you call Me good?" Jesus answered. "No one is good—except God alone. You know the commandments: Do not commit adultery, do not murder, do not steal, do not give false testimony, honor your father and your mother."

"All these instructions I have kept since I was a boy," the man responded.

When Jesus heard this He then said to him, "You still lack one thing. Sell everything you have and give it to the poor, and you will have treasure in heaven. Then come and follow Me."

When the man heard this he became very sad, because he was a man of great wealth. Jesus soon looked at him and said, "How hard it is for the rich to enter the kingdom of God! Indeed, it is easier for a camel to go through the eye of a needle than for a rich man to enter the kingdom of God."

Those who heard this asked, "Who then can be saved?"

Jesus afterward replied, "What is impossible with men is possible with God."

Luke 18:18-27

47

February 1ˢᵗ / August 1ˢᵗ

There was a man who had two sons...

The younger one said to his father, "Father, give me my share of the estate." And so the father divided his property between them. Not long after that, the younger son got together all he had, set off for a different country, and there squandered his wealth in wild living. After he had spent everything, there was a severe famine in that country, and he began to be in need.

So, he went and hired himself out to a citizen of the country, who sent him into his fields to feed pigs. The young man longed to fill his stomach with the pods that the pigs were eating, but no one would give him anything. When the lad finally came to his senses, he said, "How many of my father's hired men have food to spare, and here I am starving to death? I will set out and go back to my father and say to him: Father, I have sinned against heaven and against you. I am no longer worthy to be called your son. Make me like one of your hired men."

And so he got up and went to his father. But while he was still a long way off, his father saw the young man and was filled with compassion for him. He then ran to his son, threw his arms around him and kissed him. The son then looked into his eyes and said to him, "Father, I have sinned against heaven and against you. I am no longer worthy to be called your son."

But the father said to his servants, "Quick! Bring the best robe and put it on him. Put a ring on his finger and sandals on his feet. Bring the fatted calf and kill it. Let us have a feast and celebrate. For this son of mine was dead and is alive again; he was lost and is found!"

¤ "Come now, let us reason together," says the Lord. "Though your sins are like scarlet, they shall be as white as snow; though they are red as crimson, they shall be like wool."

Luke 15:11-24, Isaiah 1:18

February 2nd
August 2nd

Meanwhile, the elder son was in the field...

When he came near the house, he heard music and dancing. So he called one of his servants and asked him what was going on. "Your brother has come home," the servant replied, "and your father has killed the fatted calf because he has him back safe and sound."

The older brother then became angry and refused to go inside. So, his father went outside and pleaded with him. But he answered his father, "Look! All these years I have been slaving for you and never disobeyed your orders. Yet, you never gave me even a young goat so I could celebrate with my friends. But when this son of yours who has squandered your property with prostitutes comes home, you kill the fatted calf for him!"

"My son," the father then said, "you are always with me, and everything I have is yours. But we had to celebrate and be glad, because this brother of yours was dead and is alive again; he was lost and is found."

¤ Rejoice with Me; I have found My lost sheep. There will be more rejoicing in heaven over one sinner who repents than over ninety-nine righteous persons who do not need to repent.

Luke 15:25-32, Luke 15:6, 7

February 3rd / August 3rd

Manasseh was twelve years old when he became king...

He reigned in Jerusalem fifty-five years...but he did evil in the sight of the Lord, following the detestable practices of the nations that the Lord had driven out before the Israelites. He rebuilt the high places and erected alters to Baal... He bowed down to all the starry hosts and worshiped them... He sacrificed his own son in the fire, practiced sorcery and divination, and consulted with mediums and spiritists. He did much evil in the eyes of the Lord, provoking Him to anger... Moreover, Manasseh also shed so much innocent blood that he filled Jerusalem from end to end—besides the sin that he had caused Judah to commit, so that they did evil in the eyes of the Lord.

¤ The Lord spoke to Manasseh and his people, but they paid no attention. So, the Lord brought against them the army commanders of the king of Assyria, who took Manasseh prisoner, put a hook in his nose, bound him with bronze shackles and took him to Babylon. In his utter distress he sought the favor of the Lord his God and humbled himself greatly before the God of his fathers. And when he prayed to Him, the Lord was moved by the man's entreaty and listened to his plea; so He brought him back to Jerusalem and to his kingdom. Then Manasseh knew that the Lord was truly God.

¤ "No longer will a man teach his neighbor, or a man his brother, saying, 'Know the Lord,' because they will all know Me, from the least of them to the greatest," declares the Lord. "For I will forgive their wickedness, and I will extend mercy and remember their sins no more."

2nd Kings 21:1-6, 16, 2nd Chronicles:33:10-13, Jeremiah 31:34

51

February 4th / August 4th

Humble yourselves before the Lord and He will lift you up.

¤ "If My people, who are called by My name, will humble themselves, and pray and seek My face, and turn from their wicked ways, then I will hear from heaven, and will forgive their sin and heal their land," says the Lord.

¤ All of you, clothe yourselves with humility toward one another, because, God opposes the proud but gives grace to the humble. Humble yourselves, therefore, under God's mighty hand, that He may lift you up in due time. Cast all of your anxiety upon Him, because He cares for you.

¤ He performs wonders that cannot be fathomed, miracles that cannot be counted. He bestows rain on the earth; He sends water upon the countryside. The lowly He sets on high, and those who mourn are lifted to safety. ¤ The Lord sends both poverty and wealth; He humbles and He exalts. He raises the poor from the dust and lifts the needy from the ash heap; He seats them with princes and has them inherit a throne of honor.

For the foundations of the earth are the Lord's; upon them He has set the world. He will guard the feet of His saints, but the wicked will be silenced in darkness. It is not by strength that one prevails; those who oppose the Lord will be shattered.

¤ You save the humble but bring low those whose eyes are haughty. You, O Lord, keep my lamp burning; my God turns my darkness into light. With Your help I can advance against a troop; with my God I can scale a wall. As for God, His way is perfect; the word of the Lord is flawless. He is a shield for all those who take refuge in Him.

James 4:10, 2nd Chronicles 7:14, 1st Peter 5:5-7, Job 5:9-11, 1st Samuel 2:7-10, Psalm 18:27-30

February 5th / August 5th

Speak to that rock before their eyes and it will pour out its water...

¤ Jesus said, "Everyone who drinks this water will be thirsty again, but whomever drinks the water that I give them, it will become within them a spring of water welling up to eternal life. ¤ If anyone is thirsty, let him come to Me and drink. Whoever believes in Me, as the Scripture has said, streams of living water will flow from within him."

¤ The word of God is living and active. Sharper than any double-edged sword, it penetrates even to the dividing of soul and spirit, joints and marrow; it judges the thoughts and attitudes of the heart. ¤ You are a garden fountain, a well of flowing water...

¤ For God, who said, "Let light shine out of darkness," made His light shine within our hearts to give us the light of knowledge of the glory of God in the face of Christ. But, we have this treasure in jars of clay (our earthly bodies) to show that this all-surpassing power is from God and not from us.

¤ The path of the righteous is like the first gleam of dawn, shining ever brighter 'till the full light of day. ¤ You are the light of the world. A city set on a hill cannot be hidden. Neither do people light a lamp and put it under a bowl. Instead they put it on its stand, and it gives light to everyone in the house. In the same way, let your light so shine before men, that they may see your good deeds and praise your Father in heaven. ¤ ...Put on the armor of light.

Numbers 20:8, John 4:13, 14, John 7:37, 38, Hebrews 4:12, Song of Songs 4:15, 2nd Corinthians 4:6, 7, Proverbs 4:18, Matthew 5:14-16, Romans 13:12

February 6th
August 6th

Do not let the sun go down while you are still angry.

¤ If your brother sins against you, go and show him his fault, just between the two of you. If he listens to you, you have won your brother over... Then Peter came to Jesus and asked, "Lord how many times shall I forgive my brother when he sins against me?"

Jesus then answered him, "I tell you not seven times, but seventy times seven... Shouldn't you have mercy on your fellow servant, just as I have shown mercy on you?" ¤ Whatever you ask for in prayer, believe that you have received it, and it will be yours. And when you stand praying, if you hold anything against anyone, forgive him, so that your Father in heaven may forgive you of your sins.

¤ As God's chosen people, holy and dearly loved, clothe yourselves with compassion, kindness, humility, gentleness and patience. Bear with each other, and forgive one another.

¤ "No more shall every man teach his neighbor and every man teach his brother, saying, 'Know the Lord,' for they all shall know Me, from the least of them to the greatest of them," says the Lord. "For I will forgive their iniquity, and their sin I will remember no more."

Ephesians 4:26, Matthew 18:15, 21, 22, 33, Mark 11:24-26, Colossians 3:12, 13, Jeremiah 31:34

February 7th / August 7th

Every branch that bears fruit He prunes so that it will be even more fruitful.

¤ He is like a blazing fire refining precious metal, and He can bleach the dirtiest garments! Like a refiner of silver He will sit and closely watch as the dross is burned away. ¤ We can rejoice in our sufferings, because we know that suffering produces perseverance; perseverance, character; and character, hope. And hope does not disappoint...

¤ Do not make light of the Lord's discipline, and do not lose heart when He rebukes you, because the Lord disciplines those whom He loves, and He punishes everyone that He accepts as a son or daughter. Endure hardship as discipline; God is treating you as sons and daughters... No discipline seems pleasant at the time, but painful. Later on, however, it produces a harvest of righteousness and peace for those who have been trained by it.

¤ I will praise the Lord who counsels me; even at night my heart instructs me. I have set the Lord always before me. Because He is at my right hand, I will not be shaken. ¤ The precepts of the Lord are right, giving joy to the heart. The commands of the Lord are radiant, giving light to the eyes... They are more precious than gold, than much pure gold; they are sweeter than honey, than honey from the comb. By them is your servant warned; in keeping them there is great reward.

John 15:2, Malachi 3:2, 3, 5:3-5, Hebrews 12:5-7, 11,
Psalm 16:7, 8, Psalm 19:8, 10, 11

February 8th / August 8th

To some who were confident of their own righteousness and looked down on everybody else, Jesus told them this...

Two men went up to the temple to pray, one a Pharisee and the other a tax collector. The Pharisee stood up and prayed about himself: "God, I thank you that I am not like other men—robbers, evildoers, adulterers—or even like this tax collector. I fast twice a week and give a tenth of all that I get."

Yet, the tax collector stood at a distance. He would not even so much as raise his eyes to heaven, but beat on his breast and said, "God, have mercy on me, a sinner."

Jesus then said, "I tell you that this man, rather than the other, went home justified before God. For everyone who exalts himself will be humbled, and he who humbles himself will be exalted."

¤ Jesus later sat down at the place where the offerings were put and watched the crowd putting their money into the temple treasury. Many rich people threw in large amounts. But a poor widow came and put in two very small copper coins, worth only a fraction of a penny.

Calling His disciples to Him, Jesus said, "I tell you the truth, this poor widow has put more into the treasury than all the others. They all gave out of the abundance of their wealth; but she, out of her poverty, put in everything—all that she had to live on."

¤ Will the Lord be pleased with thousands of rams, or with ten thousand rivers of oil? Shall I offer my firstborn for my transgressions, the fruit of my body for the sin of my soul? He has shown you, O man, what is good. And what does the Lord require of you but to act justly, to love mercy, and to walk humbly with your God?

Luke 18:9-14, Mark 12:41-44, Micah 6:7-8

February 9th / August 9th

He led the flock to the far side of the desert and came to Horeb, the mountain of God.

¤ Then Moses went up to God, and the Lord called to him from the mountain and said, "You have seen what I did in Egypt, and how I carried you on eagles wings and brought you to Myself. Now, if you obey Me fully and keep My covenant, then out of all nations you will be My treasured possession."

¤ We know that in all things God works for the good of those who love Him, who have been called according to His purpose. For those God foreknew He also predestined to be conformed to the likeness of His Son, that He might be the firstborn among many brothers. And those He predestined, He also called; those He called, He also justified; those He justified, He also glorified. What shall we say then in response to this? If God is for us, who can be against us?

¤ The Lord is my light and my salvation; whom shall I fear?

Exodus 3:1, Exodus 19:3-5, Romans 8:28-31, Psalm 27:1

February 10th / August 10th

Teach me, O Lord, to follow Your decrees;

I will keep them to the end. Give me understanding and I will keep Your law and obey it with all my heart. Direct me in the path of Your commands, for there I find delight. Turn my heart toward Your statutes and not toward selfish gain. Turn my eyes away from worthless things; preserve my life according to Your word.

¤ Oh, how I love Your law! I meditate on it all day long. Your commands make me wiser than my enemies, for they are ever with me. I have more insight than all my teachers, for I meditate on Your statutes. I have more understanding than the elders, for I obey Your precepts... I gain understanding from Your precepts; therefore I hate every wrong path. Your word is a lamp to my feet and a light for my path... My heart is set on keeping Your decrees to the very end.

¤ The Lord is the strength of my life; of whom shall I be afraid? ...In this I will be confident.

Psalm 119:33-37, Psalm 119:97-100, 104, 105, 112, Psalm 27:1, 3

February 11th / August 11th

The law is spiritual; but I am carnal...

I do not understand what I do. For what I want to do, I do not do; but what I hate, that is what I end up doing. As it is, it is no longer I myself who does it, but it is the sin living in me—in my sinful nature. I have the desire to do what is good, but I cannot carry it out. What I end up doing is not the good that I want to do, but the evil is what I do—and I keep on doing it!

For in my inner being I delight in God's law; but I see another law at work in the members of my body, waging war against the law of my mind, and making me a prisoner of the law of sin at work in my members. What a wretched man I am! Who will rescue me from the body of this death? Thanks be to God I am rescued—through Jesus Christ our Lord!

So then, I myself in my mind am a servant of God's law, but in my sinful nature, a slave to the law of sin that resides within me. ¤ But there is no condemnation for those who are in Christ Jesus, because through Christ Jesus the law of the Spirit of life has set me free from the law of sin and death... Therefore we have an obligation—but it is not to our sinful nature, to live according to it. For if you live according to your sinful nature, you will die; but if by the Spirit you put to death the misdeeds of the body, you will live, because those who are led by the Spirit of God are the sons of God.

¤ It is for freedom that Christ has set us free. Stand firm then, and do not let yourselves be burdened again by a yoke of slavery... Live by the Spirit, and you will not gratify the desires of the sinful nature.

Romans 7:14-25, Romans 8:1, 2, 12-14,
Galatians 5:1, 16

February 12th / August 12th

And He carried me away in the Spirit to a great and high mountain...

¤ I lift up my eyes to the hills —where does my help come from? My help comes from the Lord, the maker of heaven and earth. He will not let your foot slip—He who watches over you will not slumber. ¤ There are six things the Lord hates, seven that are detestable to Him: haughty eyes, a lying tongue, hands that shed innocent blood, a heart that devises wicked schemes, feet that are quick to rush into evil, a false witness who pours out lies, and one who stirs up dissension among brothers.

¤ And I saw something else under the sun: In the place of judgment—wickedness was there, in the place of justice—wickedness was there. I thought in my heart, 'God will bring to judgment both the righteous and the wicked, for there will be a time for every activity, a time for every deed.' ¤ When you make a vow to God, do not delay in fulfilling it. He has no pleasure in fools; fulfill your vow.

¤ Go into all the world and preach the gospel to every creature. He who believes and is baptized will be saved. ¤ Then I heard the voice of the Lord saying, "Whom shall I send? And who will go for us?"—And I said, "Here am I. Send me!" He then said, "Go and tell the people..."

¤ Commit your way to the Lord; trust in Him and He will do this: He will make your righteousness shine like the dawn, the justice of your cause like the noonday sun. Be still before the Lord and wait patiently for Him.

Revelation 21:10, Psalm 121:1-3, Proverbs 6:16-19, Ecclesiastes 3:16, 17, Ecclesiastes 5:4, Mark 16:16, Isaiah 6:8, 9, Psalm 37:5-7

February 13th / August 13th

Let your gentleness be evident to all. The Lord is near.

Do not be anxious about anything, but in everything, by prayer and petition, with thanksgiving, present your requests to God. And the peace of God, which transcends all understanding, will guard your hearts and mind as you trust in Christ Jesus.

¤ The Lord Himself will come down from heaven with a loud command, with the voice of the archangel and with the trumpet call of God, and the dead in Christ will rise first. After that, we who are still alive and remain will be caught up together with them in the clouds to meet the Lord in the air. And so we will be with the Lord forever. So encourage one another with these words.

¤ In a flash, in the twinkling of an eye, at the last trumpet, the dead will be raised imperishable, and we will be changed. For the perishable must clothe itself with the imperishable, and the mortal with immorality. ¤ The sun has one kind of splendor, the moon another, and the stars another; and star differs from star in splendor. So it will be with the resurrection of the dead.

The body that is sown is perishable, it is raised imperishable; it is sown in dishonor, it is raised in glory; it is sown in weakness, it is raised in power; it is sown a natural body, it is raised a spiritual body.

Philippians 4:5-7, 1st Thessalonians 4:16-18, 1st Corinthians 15:52,53, 1st Corinthians 15:41-44

February 14th / August 14th

Come and see what God has done, how awesome His works in man's behalf!

¤ No one can look at the sun, bright as it is in the skies after the wind has swept them clean. Out of the north He comes in golden splendor; God comes in awesome majesty. The Almighty is beyond our reach and exalted in power; in His justice and great righteousness He does not oppress. Therefore men revere Him, for does He not have regard for all the wise in heart?

¤ The righteous cry out, and the Lord hears them; He delivers them from all their troubles. The Lord is close to the brokenhearted and saves those who are crushed in spirit. ¤ Let those who love the Lord hate evil, for He guards the lives of His faithful ones and delivers them from the hands of the wicked.

¤ A bruised reed He will not break, and a smoldering wick He will not snuff out... This is what the Lord God has said—He who created the heavens and stretched them out, who spread out the earth and all that comes out of it, who gives breath to its people, and life to those who walk upon it. ¤ Jesus said, "All those that the Father gives Me will come to Me, and whoever comes to Me I will never drive away."

¤ So continue then to live in Jesus, rooted and built up in Him, strengthened in the faith as you were taught, and overflowing with thankfulness. See to it that no one takes you captive through hollow and deceptive philosophy, which depends on human tradition and the basic principles of this world rather than on Christ.

Psalm 66:5, Job 37:21-24, Psalm 34:17, 18, Psalm 97:10, Isaiah 42:3, 5, John 6:37, Colossians 2:6-8

February 15th
August 15th

*My kingdom is not
of this world.*

¤ The kingdom of God does not come with your careful observation, nor will people say, "Here it is," or "There it is," because the kingdom of God is within you. ¤ Do not conform any longer to the pattern of this world, but be transformed by the renewing of your mind. Then you will be able to test and approve what God's will is—His good, pleasing and perfect will.

¤ The message of the cross is foolish to those who are perishing, but to us who are being saved it is the power of God. For it is written, 'I will destroy the wisdom of the wise; the intelligence of the intelligent I will frustrate.' Where then is the wise man? Where is the scholar? Where is the philosopher of this age? Has not God made foolish the wisdom of the world? For since in the wisdom of God the world through its wisdom did not know Him, God was pleased through the foolishness of what was preached to save those who believe.

¤ Guard what has been entrusted to you. Turn away from godless chatter and the opposing ideas of what is falsely called science and knowledge, which some have professed, and in so doing, have wandered from the faith. ¤ If one of you should wander from the truth and someone should bring him back, remember this: Whoever turns a sinner from the error of his way will save him from death and cover over a multitude of sins.

*John 18:36, Luke 17:20, 21, Romans 12:2, 1st Corinthians 1:18-21,
1st Timothy 6:20, 21, James 5:19, 20*

February 16th / August 16th

*Jesus took Peter, James and
John with Him and led them up
a high mountain, where they
were all alone...*

¤ And He taught them saying, "No good tree bears bad fruit, nor does a bad tree bear good fruit. Each tree is recognized by its own fruit. People do not pick figs from thorn bushes, nor grapes from briers. The good man brings good things out of the good stored up in his heart, and the evil man brings forth evil things out of the evil stored up in his heart. For out of the overflow of the heart the mouth speaks."

¤ When we put bits into the mouths of horses to make them obey us, we can turn the whole animal. Or take ships as an example; although they are so large and are driven by strong winds, they are steered by a very small rudder wherever the pilot wants to go.

Likewise the tongue is a small part of the body, yet it makes great boasts. Consider how a great forest is set on fire by a small spark. The tongue also is a fire—a world of evil among the parts of the body. It corrupts the whole person, sets the whole course of his/her life on fire, and is itself set on fire by hell.

All kinds of animals, birds, reptiles and creatures of the sea are being tamed and have been tamed by man, but no one can tame the tongue. It is a restless evil, full of deadly poison. ¤ I will therefore watch my ways and keep my tongue from sin; I will put a muzzle on my mouth. ¤ May my tongue sing of Your word, for all Your commands are righteous.

Mark 9:2, Luke 6:43-45, James 3:3-8, Psalm 39:1, Psalm 119:172

February 17th / August 17th

May Your hand be ready to help me, for I have chosen Your precepts.

I long for Your salvation, O Lord, and Your law is my delight. Let me live that I may praise You, and may Your laws sustain me. I have strayed like a lost sheep. Seek Your servant, for I have not forgotten Your commands.

☼ You created my inmost being; you knit me together in my mother's womb. I praise You because I am fearfully and wonderfully made;[3] Your works are wonderful, I know that full well. My frame was not hidden from You when I was made in the secret place. When I was woven together in the depths of the earth, Your eyes saw my unformed body. All the days ordained for me were written in Your book before one of them came to be. How precious to me are Your thoughts, O God. How vast is the sum of them! Were I to count them, they would outnumber the grains of sand.

☼ Yet, if only my anguish could be weighed and all my misery be placed on the scales! It would surely outweigh the sand of the seas... Oh that I might have my request, that God would grant what I hope for, that God would be willing to crush me, to let loose His hand and cut me off! Then I would still have this consolation—my joy in unrelenting pain—that I have not denied the words of the Holy One.

☼ A bruised reed He will not break, and a smoldering wick he will not snuff out. ☼ Be patient and stand firm. ☼ Do not be surprised at the painful trial you are suffering, as though some strange thing was happening to you. ☼ Know that the testing of your faith develops perseverance...that you may be mature and complete, not lacking anything.

Psalm 119:173-176, Psalm 139:13-18, Job 6:2, 3, 8-10, Matthew 12:20, James 5:8, 1ˢᵗ Peter 5:12, James 1:3, 4

67

February 18th
August 18th

Then the Lord answered Job out of the storm.

"Who is this that darkens My counsel with words without knowledge? Brace yourself like a man and I will question you. Where were you when I laid the earth's foundation? Tell me if you understand. Who marked off its dimensions? Surely you know! Who stretched a measuring line across it? On what was its footings set, or who laid its cornerstone—while the morning stars sang together and the angels shouted for joy?"

¤ The Lord reigns, let the earth be glad; let the distant shores rejoice. Clouds and thick darkness surround Him; righteousness and justice are the foundation of His throne. Fire goes before Him and consumes His foes on every side. His lightning lights up the world; the earth sees and trembles. The mountains melt like wax before the Lord, before the Lord of all the earth. The heavens proclaim His righteousness, and all the peoples see His glory.

¤ Let the sea resound, and everything in it. Let the rivers clap their hands, let the mountains sing together for joy; let them sing before the Lord, for He comes to judge the earth. He will judge the world in righteousness and the peoples with equity.

¤ I will sing of Your love and justice; to You, O Lord, I will sing praise. I will be careful to lead a blameless life—when will You come to me? ...I will have nothing to do with evil.

Job 38:1-7, Psalm 97:1-6, Psalm 98:7-9, Psalm 101:1, 2, 4

February 19ᵗʰ / August 19ᵗʰ

So Moses and Aaron said to all the Israelites, "In the evening you will know that it was the Lord who brought you out of Egypt."

¤ For He has rescued us from the dominion of darkness and brought us into the kingdom of the Son He loves, in Whom we have redemption, the forgiveness of sins. He is the image of the invisible God, the firstborn over all creation. For by Him all things were created: things in heaven and things on earth, visible and invisible, whether thrones or powers or rulers or authorities; all things were created by Him and for Him. He is before all things, and in Him all things hold together.

¤ Let it be known to you all, and to all the people of Israel, that by the name of Jesus Christ of Nazareth, whom you crucified, whom God raised from the dead, by Him this man stands here before you healed. Jesus Himself is the stone which was rejected by you builders, which has become the chief cornerstone. Nor is their salvation in any other, for there is no name under heaven given among men by which we must be saved... And with great power the apostles gave witness to the resurrection of the Lord Jesus.

¤ Jesus said, "I am the way, the truth, and the life. No one comes to the Father except through Me. ¤ Abide in Me, and I in you. As the branch cannot bear fruit of itself, unless it abides in the vine, neither can you, unless you abide in Me. I am the vine, you are the branches. He who abides in Me and I in him, bears much fruit; for without Me you can do nothing."

Exodus 16:6, Colossians 1:13-17, Acts 4:10-12, 33, John 14:6, John 15:4, 5

69

February 20th / August 20th

Trust in the Lord with all your heart, and lean not on your own understanding.

In all your ways acknowledge Him, and He shall direct your paths. Do not be wise in your own eyes; respect the Lord and depart from evil. It will be health to your flesh and strength to your bones. Honor the Lord with your possessions, and with the firstfruits of all your increase; so your barns will be filled with plenty, and your vats will overflow with new wine.

¤ To everything there is a season, a time for every purpose under heaven. A time to be born, a time to die. A time to plant, and a time to pluck up what is planted. A time to kill, and a time to heal. A time to break down, and a time to build up. A time to weep, and a time to laugh. A time to mourn, and a time to dance. A time to cast away stones, and a time to gather stones together. A time to embrace, and a time to refrain from embracing. A time to gain, and a time to lose. A time to keep, and a time to throw away. A time to tear, and a time to sew. A time to keep silent, and a time to speak. A time to love, and a time to hate. A time of war, and a time of peace.

¤ Woe to those who make unjust laws, to those who issue oppressive decrees, to deprive the poor of their rights and withhold justice from the oppressed of My people, making widows their prey and robbing the fatherless. What will you do on the day of reckoning, when disaster comes from afar? To whom will you run for help?

Proverbs 3:5-10, Ecclesiastes 3:1-8, Isaiah 10:1-3

February 21ˢᵗ / August 21ˢᵗ

I know that everything God does will endure forever;

Nothing can be added to it, and nothing taken from it. God does it so that men will revere Him. Whatever is has already been, and what will be has been before; and God will call the past to account... God will bring to judgment both the righteous and the wicked, for there will be a time for every activity, a time for every deed.

¤ Dear friends, remember what the apostles of our Lord Jesus Christ foretold. They said to you, "In these last times there will be scoffers who will follow their own ungodly ideas." These are those who divide you, who follow mere natural instincts and do not have the Spirit.

But you, dear friends, build yourselves up in your most holy faith and pray in the Holy Spirit. Keep yourselves in God's love as you wait for the mercy of our Lord Jesus Christ to bring you to eternal life. Be merciful to those who doubt; snatch others from the fire and save them; to others show mercy, mixed with fear—hating even the clothing stained by corrupted flesh.

¤ Be patient until the Lord's coming. See how the farmer waits for the land to yield its valuable crop and how patient he is for the autumn and spring rains. You too, be patient and stand firm, because the Lord's coming is near. Don't grumble at each other or you will be judged. The Judge is standing at the door.

¤ Faith is being sure of what we hope for and certain of what we do not see. It is what the ancients were commended for.

Ecclesiastes 3:14, 15, 17, Jude 17-23, James 5:7-9, Hebrews 11:1, 2

February 22nd / August 22nd

A farmer went out to sow his seed.

As he was scattering the seed, some fell by the wayside, and the birds came and ate it up. Some fell on rocky places, where there was not much soil. It sprang up quickly, because the soil was shallow. But when the sun came up, the plants were scorched, and they withered because they had no root. Other seed fell among thorns, which eventually choked the growing plants, so that they did not bear grain. Still other seed fell on good soil. It sprouted up, grew and produced a crop, multiplying thirty, sixty, and even a hundred times.

Then Jesus said to them, "Do you not understand this parable? How then will you understand all the parables? The sower sows the word of God. And these are the ones by the wayside where the word is sown: When they hear, Satan comes immediately and takes away the word that was sown in their hearts. These likewise are the ones on stony ground who, when they hear the word, immediately receive it with gladness. Yet, they have no root in themselves, and so endure only for a time. Afterward, when tribulation or persecution arises for the word's sake, immediately they stumble.

"These are the ones sown among thorns: They are the ones who hear the word, but the cares of this world, the deceitfulness of riches and the desires for other things, soon enter and choke the word, and so it becomes unfruitful. But these are the ones sown on good ground: Those who hear the word, accept it, and bear fruit; some thirty fold, some sixty, and some a hundred."

...The kingdom of God is like a mustard seed which, when it is thrown onto the ground, is smaller than all the seeds on earth. Yet, when it is sown, it grows up and becomes greater than all herbs, and shoots out large branches, so that the birds of the air may nest under its shade.

Mark 4:3-8, 13-20, 30-32

February 23rd / August 23rd

Lead me to the rock that is higher than I.

For You have been my refuge, a strong tower against the foe. I long to dwell in Your tent forever and take refuge in the shelter of Your wings. ¤ The Lord is my rock, my fortress and my deliverer; The God of my strength, in whom I will trust. I will call upon the Lord, who is worthy to be praised; So shall I be saved from my enemies.

He sent from above, He took me, He drew me out of many waters. He delivered me from my strong enemy, from those who hated me; for they were too strong for me. They confronted me in the day of my calamity, but the Lord was my support. He also brought me out into a broad place; He delivered me because He delighted in me.

¤ He alone is my rock and my salvation; He is my fortress, I will never be shaken. ¤ Oh God, You are my God, earnestly I seek You; my soul thirsts for You, my body longs for You, in a dry and weary land where there is no water... Because Your love is better than life, my lips will glorify You. I will praise You as long as I live, and in Your name I will lift up my hands.

¤ Jesus said, "Whoever comes to me and hears My sayings and does them, is like a man building a house, who dug deep and laid the foundation on a great rock. And when the flood arose, the waters beat vehemently against that house and could not shake it, for it was founded on the rock."

¤ ...and that spiritual Rock was Christ.

Psalm 61:2, 3, 2nd Samuel 22:2-4, 17-20, Psalm 62:2, Psalm 63:1,3,4, Luke 6:47, 48, 1st Corinthians 10:4

February 24ᵗʰ / August 24ᵗʰ

Why do you call me good? No one is good but One, that is, God.

¤ Have mercy upon me, O God, according to Your loving kindness; according to the multitude of Your tender mercies, blot out my transgressions. Wash me thoroughly from my iniquity, and cleanse me from my sin. For I acknowledge my transgressions, and my sin is always before me. Against You, You only, have I sinned, and done this evil in Your sight—that You may be found just when You speak, and blameless when You judge.

Behold, I was brought forth in iniquity, and in sin my mother conceived me. Surely You desire truth in the inward parts... Create in me a clean heart, O God, and renew a steadfast spirit within me... The sacrifices of God are a broken spirit, a broken and contrite heart—these, O God, you will not despise.

¤ I know that nothing good lives in me, that is, in my sinful nature. I have the desire to do what is good, but I cannot carry it out. ¤ The heart is deceitful above all things, and desperately wicked; who can understand it? ¤ What a wretched man I am! Who will rescue me from this body of death?

¤ I, the Lord, search the heart, I test the mind, to give every man according to his ways, according to the fruit of his doings. ¤ The Lord is good, a stronghold in the day of trouble; and He knows those who trust in Him.

Matthew 19:17, Psalm 51:1-6, 10, 17, Romans 7:18, Jeremiah 17:9, Romans 7:24, Jeremiah 17:10, Nahum 1:7

February 25th / August 25th

There is now no condemnation for
those who are in Christ Jesus,

who do not walk according to the flesh, but according to the Spirit. For the law of the Spirit of life in Christ Jesus has set us free from the law of sin and death. For what the law could not do, in that it was weak through the flesh, God did by sending His own Son in the likeness of sinful flesh, on account of sin: that the righteous requirement of the law might be fulfilled in us who do not walk according to the flesh but according to the Spirit...

And we know that all things work together for good to those who love God, to those who are the called according to His purpose. ¤ We who are strong ought to bear with the failings of the weak and not to please ourselves. Each of us should please his neighbor for his good, to build him up. ¤ We are regarded as servants of Christ and as those entrusted with the secret things of God. Now, it is required that those who have been given this trust must prove faithful.

¤ You are all sons of God through faith in Christ Jesus, for all of you who were baptized into Christ have clothed yourselves with Christ. There is neither Jew nor Greek, slave nor free, male nor female, for you are all one in Christ Jesus.

¤ Because of His great love for us, God, who is rich in mercy, made us alive with Christ even when we were dead in transgressions—it is by grace that you have been saved.

Romans 8:1-4, 28, Romans 15:1, 2, 1st Corinthians 4:1, 2,
Galatians 3:26-28, Ephesians 2:4, 5

February 26ᵗʰ / August 26ᵗʰ

He who forms the mountains, creates the wind, and reveals His thoughts to man; He who turns dawn to darkness, and treads the high places of the earth—the Lord Almighty is His name.

¤ The engulfing waters threatened me, the deep surrounded me; seaweed was wrapped around my head. To the roots of the mountains I sank down; the earth beneath barred me in forever. But You brought my life up from the pit, O Lord my God! When my life was ebbing away, I remembered You, Lord, and my prayer rose to You.

¤ Who is a God like You, who pardons sin and forgives the transgression of the remnant of His inheritance? You do not stay angry forever but delight to show mercy. You will again have compassion on us; You will tread our sins underfoot and hurl all of our iniquities into the depths of the sea.

¤ The Lord your God is with you, He is mighty to save. He will take great delight in you, He will quiet you with His love, He will rejoice over you with singing.

Amos 4:13, Jonah 2:5-7, Micah 7:18, 19, Zephaniah 3:17

February 27ᵗʰ / August 27ᵗʰ

No one knows about that day or hour, not even the angels in heaven, nor the Son, but only the Father.

As it was in the days of Noah, so will it be at the coming of the Son of Man. For in the days before the flood, people were eating and drinking, marrying and giving in marriage, up to the day that Noah entered the ark, and they knew nothing about what would happen until the flood came and took them all away. That is how it will be at the coming of the Son of Man.

Two men will be in the field; one will be taken and the other left. Two women will be grinding with a hand mill; one will be taken and the other left. Therefore, keep watch, because you do not know on what day your Lord will come. But understand this: If the owner of the house had known at what time of the night the thief was coming, he would have kept watch and would not have let his house be broken into. So, you also must be ready, because the Son of Man will come at an hour when you do not expect Him.

¤ The people of this age marry and are given in marriage. But those who are considered worthy of taking part in that age and in the resurrection from the dead will neither marry nor be given in marriage, and they can no longer die; for they are like the angels. They are God's children, since they are children of the resurrection.

¤ Be careful, or your hearts will be weighed down with dissipation, drunkenness and the anxieties of this life, and that day will close on you unexpectedly like a trap. For it will come upon all those who live on the face of the whole earth. Be always on the watch, and pray that you may be able to escape all that is about to happen, and that you may be able to stand before the Son of Man.

Matthew 24:36-44, Luke 20:34-36, Luke 21:34-36

79

February 28th / August 28th

*He came and preached peace to you
who were far away and peace to those
who were near.*

For through Him we both have access to the Father by one Spirit. Consequently, you are no longer foreigners and aliens, but fellow citizens with God's people and members of God's household, built on the foundation of the apostles and prophets, with Christ Jesus Himself as the chief cornerstone.

¤ Continue to work out your salvation with fear and trembling, for it is God who works in you to will and to act according to His good purpose. Do everything without complaining or arguing, so that you may become blameless and pure, children of God without fault in a crooked and depraved generation, in which you shine like stars in the universe as you hold out the word of life.

¤ Since you have been raised with Christ, set your hearts on things above, where Christ is seated at the right hand of God. Set your mind on things above and not on earthly things. For you died, and your life is now hidden with Christ in God. When Christ, who is your life, appears, then you also will appear with Him in glory.

¤ Do you not know that all of us who were baptized into Christ Jesus were baptized into His death? We were therefore buried with Him through baptism into death in order that, just as Christ was raised from the dead through the glory of the Father, we too may live a new life. If we have been united with Him in the likeness of His death, we will certainly also be united with Him in His resurrection.

*Ephesians 2:17-20, Philippians 2:12-16, Colossians 3:1-4,
Romans 6:3-5*

February 29th (Leap Year) / **August 29th**

Everything is permissible—but not everything is beneficial. Everything is permissible—but not everything is constructive.

Nobody should seek his own good, but the good of others. ¤ Evidently some people are throwing you into confusion and are trying to pervert the gospel of Christ. But even if we or an angel from heaven should preach a gospel other than the one we have preached to you, let him be eternally condemned. As we have already said, so now I say again: If anybody is preaching to you a gospel contrary to the one you were taught, let him be eternally condemned.

The gospel I preached to you is not something that man made up. I did not receive it from any man, nor was I taught it; rather, I received it by revelation from Jesus Christ. ¤ All Scripture is God-breathed and is useful for teaching, rebuking, correcting and training in righteousness, so that the man/woman of God may be thoroughly equipped for every good work.

¤ It is better to trust in the Lord than to put confidence in man.[4] It is better to take refuge in the Lord than to trust in princes. ¤ Deliver me, O Lord, from evil men; preserve me from violent men, who plan evil things in their hearts. They continually gather together for war. They sharpen their tongues like a serpent; the poison of asps is under their lips. Keep me, O Lord, from the hands of the wicked... You are the strength of my salvation. ¤ He who trusts in himself is a fool, but he who trusts in the Lord will prosper.

1st Corinthians 10:23, 24, Galatians 1:7-9, 11, 12,
2nd Timothy 3:16, 17, Psalm 118:8, 9,
Psalm 140:1-4, 7, Proverbs 28:26

August 30th

When a country is rebellious, it has many rulers, but a man of understanding and knowledge maintains order.

A ruler who oppresses the poor is like a driving rain that leaves no crops.

Those who forsake the law praise the wicked, but those who keep the law resist them. Evil men do not understand justice, but those who seek the Lord understand it fully.

Better a poor man whose walk is blameless than a rich man whose ways are perverse... He who increases his wealth by exorbitant interest amasses it for another, who will be kind to the poor... A rich man may be wise in his own eyes, but a poor man who has discernment sees through him.

When the righteous triumph, there is great elation; but when the wicked rise to power, men go into hiding. He who conceals his sins does not prosper, but whoever confesses and renounces them finds mercy. Blessed is the man who always fears the Lord, but he who hardens his heart falls into trouble.

¤ Your statutes are wonderful; therefore I obey them. The unfolding of Your words give light; it gives understanding to the simple. I open my mouth and pant, longing for Your commands. Turn to me and have mercy on me, as You always do those who love Your name. Direct my footsteps according to Your word; let no sin rule over me.

Proverbs 28:2-6, 8, 11-14, Psalm 119:129-133

August 31st

Now, son of man, set your face against the daughters of your people who prophesy out of their own imagination.

This is what the Sovereign Lord says: "Woe to the women who sew magic charms on all their wrists and make veils of various lengths for their heads in order to ensnare people. Will you ensnare the lives of My people but preserve your own? And woe to the foolish prophets who follow their own spirit and have seen nothing. Your prophets are like jackals among ruins."

¤ Yes, there were false prophets among the ancients, both male and female, just as there will be false teachers among you. They will secretly induce destructive heresies, even denying the Sovereign Lord—bringing swift destruction upon themselves. Many will follow their shameful ways and will bring the way of truth into disrepute... But their condemnation has long been hanging over them, and their destruction has not been sleeping... They are springs without water, and mists driven by a storm.

¤ Beware of false prophets...You will know them by their fruits.

Ezekiel 13:17, 18, Ezekiel 13:3, 4, 2nd Peter 2:1-3, 17, Matthew 7:15, 16

March 1st
September 1st

Go out and stand on the mountain in the presence of the Lord, for the Lord is about to pass by.

Then a great and powerful wind tore into the mountains and broke the rocks in pieces before the Lord, but the Lord was not in the wind; and after the wind an earthquake, but the Lord was not in the earthquake; and after the earthquake a fire erupted, but the Lord was not in the fire. And after the fire came a still, small voice. When Elijah heard it he pulled his cloak about his face and went out and stood at the mouth of the cave.

Then the voice said to him, "What are you doing here, Elijah?" The man then replied, "I have been very zealous for the Lord God Almighty. The Israelites have rejected Your covenant, broken down Your alters, and put Your prophets to death with the sword. I am the only one left, and now they are trying to kill me too."

The Lord then said to him, "Go back the way you came... I have reserved seven thousand in Israel—all whose knees have not bowed to Baal, and all whose mouths have not kissed him." ¤ At the sight of his friends Paul thanked God and was encouraged. ¤ Jesus said, "Where two or three come together in My name, there I am with them." ¤ Be strong and of good courage... The Lord is the One who goes with you; He will never leave you nor forsake you.

1st Kings 19:11-15, 18, Acts 28:15, Matthew 18:20, Deuteronomy 31:6

March 2nd / September 2nd

I will not forget you! See, I have engraved you on the palms of My hands.

¤ The Lord is good, a stronghold in the day of trouble; and He knows those who trust in Him. ¤ This is what the Lord says, "Heaven is My throne, and the earth is My footstool... Has not My hand made all these things, and so they came into being? This is the one whom I esteem: He who is humble and contrite in spirit, and trembles at My word."

¤ Praise be to the name of God for ever and ever; wisdom and power are His. He changes times and seasons; He sets up kings and disposes them. He gives wisdom to the wise and knowledge to the discerning. He reveals deep and hidden things; He knows what lies in darkness, and light dwells within Him.

¤ In all things we are more than conquerors through Him who loved us. For I am convinced that neither death nor life, neither angels nor demons, neither the present nor the future, nor any powers, neither height nor depth, nor anything else in all creation, will be able to separate us from the love of God that is in Christ Jesus our Lord.

¤ For He chose us in Him before the creation of the world to be holy and blameless in His sight. In love He predestined us to be adopted as His sons through Jesus Christ, in accordance with His pleasure and will... In Him we have redemption through His blood, the forgiveness of sins, in accordance with the riches of God's grace.

*Isaiah 49:15, 16, Nahum 1:7, Isaiah 66:1, 2, Daniel 2:20-22,
Romans 8:37-39, Ephesians 1:4, 5, 7*

March 3rd / September 3rd

For you were once darkness, but now you are the light of the world.

Live as children of light (for the fruit of the light consists in all goodness, righteousness and truth) and find out what pleases the Lord. Have nothing to do with the fruitless deeds of darkness, but rather expose them. For it is shameful even to mention what the disobedient do in secret. But everything exposed by the light becomes visible, for it is light that makes everything visible. This is why it is said, "Wake up, O sleeper, rise from the dead and Christ will shine on you."

Be careful then how you live—not as unwise but as wise, making the most of every opportunity, because the days are evil.

¤ Light has come into the world, but men loved darkness instead of light because their deeds were evil. Everyone who does evil hates the light, and will not come into the light for fear that his deeds will be exposed. But whoever lives by the truth comes into the light, so that it may be seen plainly that what he has done has been done through God.

¤ To those who had believed on Him, Jesus said, "If you hold to My teaching, you are truly My disciples. Then you will know the truth, and the truth will set you free... I tell you the truth, everyone who sins is a slave to sin. Now a slave has no permanent place in the family, but a son belongs to it forever. So if the Son sets you free, you will be free indeed. ¤ You are the light of the world."

Ephesians 5:8-16, John 3:19-21, John 8:31, 32, 34-36, Matthew 5:14

86

March 4th / September 4th

Blessed are the humble in spirit, for theirs is the kingdom of heaven.

Blessed are those who mourn, for they will be comforted.
Blessed are the meek, for they will inherit the earth.
Blessed are those who hunger and thirst for what is right, for they will be filled.
Blessed are the merciful, for they will be shown mercy.
Blessed are the pure in heart, for they will see God.
Blessed are the peacemakers, for they will be called the sons of God.
Blessed are those who are persecuted for doing what is right, for theirs is the kingdom of heaven.
Blessed are you when people insult you, persecute you and falsely say all kinds of evil against you because of Jesus. I say rejoice and be glad, because great is your reward in heaven, for in the very same way they persecuted the prophets who lived long before you.

You are the salt of the earth. But if the salt loses its saltiness, how can it me made salty again? It is no longer good for anything, except to be thrown out and trampled by men. You are the light of the world. A city on a hill cannot be hidden. Neither do people light a lamp and put it under a bowl. Instead they put it on its stand, and it gives light to everyone in the house. In the same way, let your light shine before men, that they may see your good deeds and praise your Father in heaven.

Matthew 5:3-16

March 5th / September 5th

I guide you in the way of wisdom and lead you along straight paths.

When you walk, your steps will not be hampered; when you run, you will not stumble. Hold on to instruction, do not let it go; guard it well, for it is your life. Do not set foot on the path of the wicked or walk in the way of evil men. Avoid it, do not travel on it; turn from it and go on your way... The path of the righteous is like the first gleam of dawn, shining ever brighter until the full light of day. But the way of the wicked is like deep darkness; they do not know what makes them stumble.

My son, pay attention to what I say; listen closely to My words. Do not let them out of your sight, keep them within your heart; for they are life to those who find them and health to a man's whole body. Above all else guard your heart, for it is the wellspring of life. Put away perversity from your mouth; keep corrupt talk from your lips. Let your eyes look straight ahead, fix your gaze directly before you. Make level paths for your feet and take only ways that are firm. Do not swerve to the right or the left; keep your foot from evil.

Proverbs 4:11-15, 18-27

March 6th / September 6th

*The two angels arrived at
Sodom in the evening.*

"My lords," Lot said, "please
turn aside to your servant's house."
He insisted strongly and the angels
went with him and entered the
house, where Lot prepared a meal for them. Not long afterward, all the men from every part of the city of Sodom—both young and old—surrounded the house.

They soon called out to Lot,"Where are the men who came to you tonight? Bring them out to us so that we can have sex with them."

Lot then went outside to meet them and shut the door behind him, and said, "No, my friends. Don't do this wicked thing. Look, I have two daughters who have never slept with a man. Let me bring them out to you and you can do what you like with them. But don't do anything to my two guests, for they have come under the protection of my roof."

"Get out of our way," the mob replied in anger. And they said, "This fellow came here as a foreigner, and now he wants to play judge! We'll treat you worse than them." The people kept bringing pressure on Lot and moved forward to break down the door of the house.

But the angels inside reached out and pulled Lot back into the house and shut the door. Then they struck the men who were at the door of the house, young and old, with blindness so that they could not find the door... With the coming of dawn the angels urged Lot, saying, "Hurry! Take you wife and your two daughters who are here and flee to the mountains, or you will be swept away when the city is punished."

Genesis 19:1-11, 15

March 7th
September 7th

By the time Lot reached Zoar the sun had risen over the land.

Then the Lord rained down burning sulfur on Sodom and Gomorrah—from the Lord out of the heavens. Thus He overthrew those cities and the entire plain, including all those living in the cities... ¤ He condemned the cities of Sodom and Gomorrah by burning them to ashes, and made them an example of what is going to happen to the ungodly.

Yet, He rescued Lot from among them, a righteous man, who was distressed by the filthy lives of lawless men, his soul tormented by their shameful deeds. If this is so, then the Lord knows how to rescue godly men from trials and to hold the unrighteousness for the day of judgment, while continuing their punishment. This is especially true of those who follow the corrupt desires of the sinful nature.

¤ Even their women exchanged natural relations for unnatural ones. In the same way the men also abandoned natural relations with women, and were inflamed with lust for one another. Men committed indecent acts with other men, and received in themselves the due penalty for their perversion. ¤ Flee from sexual immorality. All other sins that one commits are outside the body, but those who commit acts of sexual perversion sin against their own bodies.

Genesis 19:22-25, 2nd Peter 2:6-10, Romans 1:26, 27,
1st Corinthians 6:18

March 8th / September 8th

The Lord said to Moses...

"Speak to the people and say to them: 'I am the Lord your God. You must not do as they do in Egypt, where you use to live, and you must not do as they do in the land of Canaan, where I am bringing you. Do not follow their practices...
'Do not have sexual relations with your neighbor's wife and defile yourself with her... Do not lie with a man as one lies with a woman; that is detestable. Do not have sexual relations with an animal and defile yourself with it. A woman must not present herself to an animal to have sexual relations with it; that is perversion.
'Do not defile yourselves in any of these ways, because this is how the nations that I am going to drive out before you became defiled. Even the land was defiled; so I punished it for its sin, and the land vomited out its inhabitants.
'The native born and the foreigners living among you must not do any of these detestable things, for all these things were done by the people who lived in the land before you, and the land became defiled. And if you defile the land, it will vomit you out as it vomited out the nations that were before you.'"

Leviticus 18:1-4, 20, 22-28

91

March 9th / September 9th

For unto us a child is born, unto us a Son is given;

And the government will be upon His shoulder. His name will be called Wonderful, Counselor, the Mighty God, the Everlasting Father, the Prince of Peace. Of the increase of His government and peace there will be no end.

¤ All things were made through Him, and without Him nothing was made that was made. In Him was life, and the life was the light of men. And the light shines in the darkness, and the darkness did not comprehend it.

¤ Oh, the depth of the riches both of the wisdom and knowledge of God! How unsearchable are His judgments and His ways past finding out! For who has known the mind of the Lord? Or who has become His counselor? Or who has first given to God that God should repay him? For of Him and through Him and to Him are all things. To Him be glory forever.

¤ We know that we have come to know Him, if we obey His commands... The word of God lives in you.

Isaiah 9:6, 7, John 1:3-5, Romans 11:33-36, 1st John 2:3, 14

92

March 10ᵗʰ / September 10ᵗʰ

The people come near to Me with their mouth and honor Me with their lips, but their hearts are far from Me.

Their worship of Me is made up only of rules taught by men. Therefore once more I will astound these people with wonder upon wonder; the wisdom of the wise will perish, the intelligence of the intelligent will vanish. Woe to those who go to great depths to hide their plans from the Lord, who do their work in darkness and think, "Who sees us? Who will know?"

They turn things upside down, as if the Potter were thought to be like the clay! Shall what is formed say to Him who formed it, "He did not make me?" Can the pot say of the Potter, "He knows nothing?" ¤ As water reflects a face, so a man's heart reflects the man. Death and destruction are never satisfied, and neither are the eyes of a man.

¤ He who conceals his sins does not prosper, but whoever confesses and renounces them finds mercy. Blessed is the man who always fears the Lord, but he who hardens his heart falls into trouble. ¤ Let us then acknowledge the Lord; let us press on to acknowledge Him. As surely as the sun rises, He will appear; He will come to us like the winter rains, like the spring rains that water the earth.

¤ Does the hawk take flight by your wisdom? ¤ The Lord is your refuge and your fortress; the God in whom you can trust... He will cover you with His feathers, and under His wings you will find refuge.

Isaiah 29:13-16, Proverbs 27:19, 20, Provers 28:13, 14,
Hosea 6:3, Job 39:26, Psalm 91:2, 4

March 11ᵗʰ / September 11ᵗʰ

You must teach what is in accord with sound doctrine.

Teach the older men to be temperate, worthy of respect, self-controlled, and sound in faith, in love and endurance. Likewise, teach the older women to be reverent in the way they live, not to be slanderers or addicted to much wine, but to teach what is good. Then they can train the younger women to love their husbands and children, to be self-controlled and pure, to be busy at home, to be kind, and to be subject to their husbands, so that no one will malign the word of God.

Similarly, encourage the young men to be self-controlled. In everything set them an example by doing what is good. In your teaching show integrity, seriousness and soundness of speech that cannot be condemned... For the grace of God that brings salvation has appeared to all men. It teaches us to say "No" to ungodliness and worldly passions, and to live self-controlled, upright and godly lives in this present age, while we wait for the blessed hope—the glorious appearing of our great God and Savior, Jesus Christ, who gave Himself to redeem us from all wickedness and to purify for Himself a people that are His very own, eager to do what is good.

These, then, are the things you should teach. Encourage and rebuke with all authority. Do not let anyone despise you. Remind the people to be subject to rulers and authorities, to be obedient, to be ready to do whatever is good, to slander no one, to be peaceable and considerate, and to show true humility toward all men.

Titus 2:1-8, 11-15, & Titus 3:1, 2

94

March 12ᵗʰ / September 12ᵗʰ

*When Christ came into the world,
He said this to God the Father:*

"Sacrifice and offering You did not desire, but a body You prepared for Me; with burnt offerings and sin offerings You were not pleased. Then I said, 'Here am I—it is written about Me in the scroll—I have come to do Your will, O God.'"

First He said, "Sacrifices and offerings, burnt offerings and sin offerings You did not desire, nor were You pleased with them" (although the law required them to be made). Then He said, "Here I am, I have come to do Your will." He sets aside the first to establish the second. And by that will, we have been made holy through the sacrifice of the body of Jesus Christ once and for all.

¤ Therefore contend for the faith that was once for all entrusted to the saints. ¤ There is one God and one mediator between God and men, the man Christ Jesus, who gave Himself as a ransom for all men—a testimony given in its proper time. ¤ There is one body and one Spirit—just as you were called to one hope when you were called—one Lord, one faith, one baptism, one God and Father of all, who is over all and though all and in all.

But to each one of us grace has been given as Christ apportioned it. This is why it says: "When He ascended on high, He led captives in His train and gave gifts to men."

Hebrews 10:5-10, Jude 3, 1ˢᵗ Timothy 2:5, 6, Ephesians 4:4-8

March 13th / September 13th

Show me your faith without deeds, and I will show you my faith by what I do.

Do you believe that there is one God? Good! Even the demons believe that—and shudder. You foolish man, do you want evidence that faith without deeds is useless? Was not Abraham considered righteous for what he did when he offered his son Isaac on the alter? You can see that his faith and his actions were working together, and his faith was made complete by what he did...

You see then that a person is justified by what he or she does and not by faith alone... As the body without the spirit is dead, so faith without accompanying deeds is also dead. ¤ We know that God does not listen to sinners. He listens to the godly man who does His will. ¤ Jesus said, "Why do you call Me, 'Lord, Lord,' and do not what I say?"

James 2:18-22, 24, 26, John 9:31, Luke 6:46

96

March 14th
September 14th

John's disciples came to Jesus and asked of Him...

"Are You the One who was to come, or should we expect someone else?" At that very time Jesus cured many who had diseases, sicknesses, and evil spirits, and gave sight to many who were blind. And so He replied to John's messengers:

"Go back and report to John what you have seen and heard: The blind receive sight, the lame walk, those who have leprosy are cured, the deaf hear, the dead are raised, and the good news is preached to the poor. Blessed is the man who does not fall away on account of Me."

After John's messengers left, Jesus began to speak to the crowd about John: "What did you go out into the desert to see? A reed swayed by the wind? If not, what did you go out to see? A man dressed in fine clothes? No, those who wear expensive clothes and indulge in luxury are living in palaces. But what did you go out to see? A Prophet? Yes, I tell you, and more than a prophet. This is one about whom it is written:

"'I will send My messenger ahead of You, who will prepare Your way before You.' I tell you, among those born of women there is no one greater than John the baptist; yet the one who is the very least in the kingdom of God is greater than he. ¤ And there are some of you standing here right now that will not taste of death before they see the kingdom of God come with power."

Luke 7:18-28, Mark 9:1

March 15th / September 15th

And He gave instruction to the apostles He had chosen...

"Do not leave Jerusalem, but wait for the gift My Father has promised, which you have heard Me speak about. For John baptized with water, but in a few days you will be baptized with the Holy Spirit... You will receive power when the Holy Spirit comes upon you; and you will be My witnesses in Jerusalem, and in all Judea and Samaria, and to the ends of the earth."

¤ When the day of Pentecost had come, they were all together in one place. Suddenly a sound like the blowing of a violent wind came from heaven and filled the whole house where they were sitting. They saw what seemed to be tongues of fire that separated and came to rest upon each of them. The twelve were then filled with the Holy Spirit and began to speak in other languages as the Spirit enabled them.

Now there were staying in Jerusalem God-fearing Jews from every nation under heaven. When they heard this sound, the crowd came together in bewilderment, because each one heard them speaking in his own language... Then Peter stood up with the eleven, raised his voice and addressed the crowd...

When the people heard all that he had said regarding the crucifixion, death, burial and resurrection of Jesus, they were cut to the heart, and soon said to Peter and the rest of the apostles, "Brothers, what shall we do?"

Acts1:1:2, 4, 5, 8, Acts 2:1-6, 14, 37

March 16th / September 16th

Peter stood before the crowd and responded.

"Repent and be baptized, every one of you, in the name of Jesus Christ for the forgiveness of your sins. And you will then receive the gift of the Holy Spirit. The promise is for you and your children, and for all who are far off—for all whom the Lord our God will call."

With many other words he warned them; and he pleaded with them, "Save yourselves from this corrupt generation." And those who believed and accepted his message were baptized, and about three thousand were added to their number that day. These people devoted themselves to the apostles teaching and to fellowship, to the breaking of bread, and to prayer. Everyone was filled with awe, and many wonders and miraculous signs were done by the apostles.

All the believers were together and had everything in common. Selling their possessions and goods, they kindly gave to anyone as he/she had need. Everyday they continued to meet together in the temple courts. They also broke bread in their homes and ate together with glad and sincere hearts, praising God and having favor with all the people. And the Lord added to the church daily those who were being saved.

¤ Whosoever believes and is baptized will be saved.

Acts 2:38-47, Mark 16:16

March 17th / September 17th

Be steadfast and immovable...

¤ If you have believed on Christ Jesus as Lord, continue to live in Him, rooted and built up in Him, strengthened in the faith as you were taught, and overflowing with thankfulness. See to it that no one takes you captive through hollow and deceptive philosophy, which depends on human tradition and the basic principles of this world rather than on Christ.

¤ I pray that out of His glorious riches He may strengthen you with power through His Spirit in your inner being, so that Christ may dwell in your hearts through faith. And I pray that you, being rooted and established in love, may have power together with all the saints, to grasp how wide and long and high and deep is the love of Christ, and to know this love that surpasses knowledge—that you may be filled to the measure of all the fullness of God.

¤ Trust in the Lord with all your heart, and lean not on your own understanding. In all your ways acknowledge Him, and he shall direct your paths. ¤ Blessed is the man who does not walk in the counsel of the wicked nor stand in the path of sinners nor sit in the seat of mockers. But his delight is in the Law of the Lord, and on His law he meditates day and night. He is like a tree planted by the rivers of water, that brings forth its fruit in its season, whose leaf also shall not wither; and whatever he does shall prosper.

1st Corinthians 15:58, Colossians 2:6-8, Ephesians 3:16-19, Proverbs 3:5, 6, Psalm 1:1-3

March 18th / September 18th

Answer me when I call to You...

O, my righteous God. Give me relief from my distress; be merciful to me and hear my prayer... Know that the Lord has set apart the godly for Himself; the Lord will hear when I call to Him. In your anger do not sin; when you are on your beds, search your hearts and be silent. Offer right sacrifices and trust in the Lord.

¤ The sacrifices of God are a broken spirit; a broken and contrite heart, O God, You will not despise. ¤ Let me sit alone in silence, for You have laid it upon me. Let me bury my face in the dust—there may yet be hope. ¤ May Your unfailing love come to me, O Lord; Your salvation according to Your promise.

¤ How precious to me are Your thoughts toward me, O God! How vast is the sum of them! Were I to count them, they would outnumber the grains of sand on the seashore. ¤ Who has measured the waters in the hollow of his hand, or with the breadth of his hand marked off the heavens? Who has held the dust of the earth in a basket, or weighed the mountains on the scales and the hills in a balance?

Who has directed the Spirit of the Lord, or as His counselor has guided Him? With whom did He take counsel, and who instructed Him and taught Him the path of justice? Who taught Him knowledge, and showed Him the way of understanding? Surely the nations of men are like a drop in a bucket; they are regarded as dust on the scales. ¤ It is better to take refuge in the Lord than to trust in man.[4]

Psalm 4:1, 3-5, Psalm 51:17, Lamentations 3:28, 29, Psalm 119:41, Psalm 139:17, 18, Isaiah 40:12-15, Psalm 118:8

March 19th
September 19th

Thanks be to God for His indescribable gift!

¤ We always thank God, the Father of our Lord Jesus Christ, when we pray for you, because we have heard of your faith in Christ and of the love you have for all the saints—the faith and love that spring from the hope that is stored up for you in heaven, and that you have already heard about in the word of truth, the gospel that has come to you. All over the world this gospel is bearing fruit and growing, just as it has been doing among you since the day you heard it and understood God's grace in all of its truth.

¤ You are all sons of God through faith in Christ Jesus, for all of you who were baptized into Christ have clothed yourselves with Christ. There is neither Jew nor Greek, slave nor free, male nor female, for you are all one in Christ Jesus.

¤ So I say, live by the Spirit, and you will not gratify the desires of the sinful nature. For the sinful nature desires what is contrary to the Spirit, and the Spirit what is contrary to the sinful nature. These two are in conflict with one another, so that you do not do what you want to do. But if you are led by the Spirit, you are not under law... The fruit of the Spirit is love, joy, peace, patience, kindness, goodness, faithfulness, gentleness, and self-control. Against such things there is no law.

2nd Corinthians 9:15, Colossians 1:1-6, Galatians 3:26-28, Galatians 5:16-18, 22, 23

March 20th
September 20th

I run not with uncertainty...

I fight not as one who just beats the air, but I discipline my body and bring it into subjection. ¤ I have fought the good fight, I have finished the race, I have kept the faith. Now there is in store for me a crown of righteousness, which the Lord, the righteous Judge, will award to me on that day—and not to me only, but also to all those who have longed for His appearing.

¤ If someone is caught in a sin, you who are spiritual should restore him/her gently. But watch yourself, or you also may be tempted. Carry each others burdens, and in this way you will fulfill the law of Christ. If anyone thinks he/she is something when they are nothing, they deceive themselves. Each one should test their own actions. Then they can then take pride in themselves without comparing themselves to anyone else, for each one should carry his/her own load.

¤ The Spirit searches all things, even the deep things of God. For who among men or women knows the thoughts of a man or a woman except the individual person's spirit within them? In the same way, no one knows the thoughts of God except the Spirit of God. Yet we have not received the spirit of the world, but the Spirit who is from God, that we may come to understand what God has freely given us.

¤ The life I now live in the body, I live by faith in the Son of God, who loved me and gave Himself for me.

1st Corinthians 9:26, 27, 2nd Timothy 4:7, 8, Galatians 6:1-5, 1st Corinthians 2:10-12, Galatians 2:20

103

March 21st / September 21st

Bear with each other...

And forgive whatever grievances you may have against one another. Forgive as the Lord forgave you. ¤ The Lord is merciful and gracious, slow to anger and abounding in mercy. He will not always strive with us, nor will He keep His anger forever. He has not dealt with us according to our sins, nor punished us according to our iniquities.

For as the heavens are high above the earth, so great is His mercy toward those who fear Him; as far as the east is from the west, so far He has removed our transgressions from us. As a father pities his children, so the Lord pities those who fear Him. For He knows our frame; He remembers that we are but dust.

As for man, his days are like grass; as a flower of the field, so he flourishes. For the wind passes over it, and it is gone, and its place remembers it no more. But the mercy of the Lord is from everlasting to everlasting on those who fear Him. ¤ Do not be wise in your own eyes. Fear the Lord and depart from evil.

¤ Jesus said to his disciples: "Things that cause people to sin are bound to come, but woe to that person through whom they do come. It would be better for him to be thrown into the sea with a millstone tied around his neck than for him to cause another to sin. So watch yourselves.

"If your brother sins, rebuke him, and if he repents, forgive him. If he sins against you seven times a day, and seven times comes back to you, and says, 'I repent,' then forgive him."

Colossians 3:13, Psalm 103:8-17, Proverbs 3:7, Luke 17:1-4

March 22nd / September 22nd

And Jesus was tempted in the wilderness...

The devil said to Him, "If You are the Son of God, then command this stone to become bread." But Jesus answered him, saying, "It is written, 'Man shall not live by bread alone, but by every word of God.'"

Then the devil, taking Him up on a high mountain, showed Him all the kingdoms of the world in a moment of time. And the devil said to Him, "All their authority and splendor I will give to You; for all this has been given to me, and I can give it to whomever I wish. So, if You worship me, it will all be yours."

Jesus then answered, "It is written: 'Worship the Lord your God and serve Him only.'"

The devil afterward led Him to Jerusalem and had Him stand on the highest point of the temple. He then said, "If You are the Son of God, throw yourself down from here. For it is written: 'He will command His angels concerning You to guard You carefully; they will lift You in their hands, so that You will not strike Your foot against a stone.'"

Jesus answered, "It also says: 'Do not put the Lord your God to the test.'"

When the devil had finished all this tempting, he left Jesus until an opportune time.

¤ Put on the full armor of God so that you can take your stand against the devil's schemes. For our personal struggles are not against flesh and blood; but against the rulers, against the authorities, against the powers of this dark world, and against the spiritual forces of evil in the heavenly realms.

Luke 4:1-13, Ephesians 6:11, 12

March 23rd / September 23rd

The Lord is near. Do not be anxious about anything.

In everything, by prayer, petition and thankfulness, present your requests to God. And the peace of God, which passes all understanding, will guard your hearts and minds as you trust in Christ Jesus. ¤ Are not two sparrows sold for a penny? Yet not one of them will fall to the ground apart from the will of your Father. And even the very hairs of your head are numbered. So don't be afraid; you are more valuable than many sparrows.

¤ You are a shield around me, O Lord; You bestow glory on me and lift up my head. ¤ In the morning, O Lord, You hear my voice; in the morning I lay my requests before You and wait in expectation... Let all who take refuge in You be glad; let them ever sing for joy. Spread Your protection over them, that those who love Your name may rejoice in You. For surely, O Lord, You bless the righteous; You surround them with Your favor as with a shield.

¤ The Lord has chastened me severely, but He has not given me over to death. ¤ Blessed is the man whom God corrects; so do not despise the discipline of the Almighty. For He wounds, but He also binds up; He injures, but His hands also heal. From six calamities He will rescue you; in seven no harm will befall you. In famine He will ransom you from death, and in battle from the stroke of the sword. You will be protected from the lash of the tongue, and need not fear when destruction comes.

¤ Have no fear then of sudden disaster or of the ruin that overtakes the wicked, for the Lord will be your confidence, and will keep your foot from being snared.

Philippians 4:6, 7, Matthew 10:29-31, Psalm 3:3, Psalm 5:3, 11, 12, Psalm 118:18, Job 5:17-21, Proverbs 3:25, 26

March 24th / September 24th

Before the mountains were settled in place, before the hills, I was given birth.

¤ How many are Your works, O Lord! In wisdom You made them all; the earth is full of Your creations. ¤ I, wisdom, dwell with prudence; I possess knowledge and discretion... Counsel and sound judgment are mine; I have understanding and power... The Lord brought me forth as the first of His works, before His deeds of old. I was appointed from eternity, before the world even began... Listen to my instruction and be wise; do not ignore it... For whoever finds me finds life and receives favor from the Lord.

¤ And Jesus grew into manhood and became strong; He was filled with wisdom, and the grace of God was upon Him.

¤ The message of the cross is foolishness to those who are perishing, but to us who are being saved it is the power of God. For it is written: "I will destroy the wisdom of the wise; the intelligence of the intelligent I will frustrate."

Where is the wise man? Where is the scholar? Where is the philosopher of this age? Has not God made foolish the wisdom of the world? For since in the wisdom of God the world through its wisdom did not know Him, God was pleased through the so-called 'foolishness' of what was preached to save those who will believe.

Proverbs 8:25, Psalm 104:24, Proverbs 8:12, 14, 22, 23, 33, 35, Luke 2:40, 1st Corinthians 1:18-21

107

March 25th September 25th

*We speak a message of
wisdom among the mature.*

It is not the wisdom of this age or of the rulers of this age, who are coming to nothing. No, we speak of God's secret wisdom, a wisdom that has been hidden and that God destined for our glory before time began. None of the rulers of this age understood it, for if they had, they would not have crucified the Lord of glory.

However, as it is written: "No eye has seen, no ear has heard, no mind has conceived what God has prepared for those who love Him." But, God has revealed it to us by His Spirit.

¤ Jesus said, "I am the true vine, and My Father is the gardener. He cuts off every branch in Me that bears no fruit, while every branch that does bear fruit He prunes so that it will be even more fruitful. You are already clean because of the word I have spoken to you. Remain in Me, and I will remain in you. No branch can bear fruit by itself; it must remain in the vine. Neither can you bear fruit unless You remain in Me.

I am the vine; you are the branches. If a person remains in Me and I in them, they will bear much fruit, for apart from Me you can do nothing. If anyone does not remain in Me, he is like a branch that is thrown away and withers; such branches are picked up, thrown into the fire and burned. If you remain in Me and My words remain in you, ask whatever you wish, and it will be given you. This is to My Father's glory, that you bear much fruit, showing yourselves to be My disciples."

1st Corinthians 2:6-10, John 15:1-8

March 26th / September 26th

If the world hates you, know that it hated Me before it hated you.

If you belonged to the world, it would love you as its own. As it is, you do not belong to the world, but I have chosen you out of the world. That is why the world hates you. Remember the words that I have spoken to you: 'No servant is greater than his master.' If they persecuted Me, they will persecute you also...

They will treat you this way because of My name, for they do not know the One who sent Me. If I had not come and spoken to them, they would not be guilty of sin. Now, however, they have no excuse for their sin. He who hates Me hates My Father as well. If I had not done among them the works that no one else did, they would have no sin. But now they have seen the miracles, and yet they have hated both Me and My Father. But this happened to fulfill what is written in their law: 'They hated me without a cause.' ¤ These things I have spoken to you, that you should not be made to stumble... And these things they will do to you because they have not known the Father nor Me.

¤ And there will be signs in the sun, moon and stars. On the earth, nations will be in perplexity at the roaring and tossing of the sea. Men will faint from terror, apprehensive of what is coming on the world, for the heavenly bodies will be shaken. At that time they will see the Son of Man coming in a cloud with power and great glory. When these things begin to take place, stand up and lift up your heads, because your redemption is drawing near. ¤ He is coming with the clouds, and every eye shall see Him.

John 15:18-25, John 16:1, 3, Luke 21:25-28, Revelation 1:7

March 27th / September 27th

*Go into all the world and preach
the good news to all creation.*

Whoever believes and is baptized will be saved, but whoever does not believe will be condemned. ¤ I tell you the truth, no one can enter the kingdom of God unless he/she is born of water and the Spirit. You should not be surprised at My saying, 'You must be born again.' The wind blows wherever it pleases. You hear its sound, but you cannot tell where it comes from nor where it is going. So it is with everyone who is born of the Spirit.

¤ Repent and be baptized, every one of you, in the name of Jesus Christ for the forgiveness of your sins. And you will receive the gift of the Holy Spirit. This promise is for you and your children and for all who are far off—for all whom the Lord our God will call... Those who accepted his message were baptized, and about three thousand were added to their number that day.

¤ Now as Phillip and the Ethiopian eunuch traveled down the road, they came to some water. And the eunuch said, "See, here is water. What hinders me from being baptized?"

Then Philip said, "If you believe with all of your heart, you may." And so the eunuch answered and said, "I believe that Jesus Christ is the Son of God."

So he commanded the chariot to stand still. And both Philip and the eunuch went down into the water and Philip baptized him. Now when they came up out of the water, the Spirit of the Lord caught Philip away, so that the eunuch saw him no more. The eunuch then went on his way rejoicing!

Mark !6:16, 17, John 3:5-8, Acts 2:38, 39, 41, Acts 8:36-39

110

March 28th / September 28th

The God of our fathers has chosen you...

That you should know His will, and see the Righteous One, and hear the voice of His mouth. For you will be His witness to all men and women of what you have seen and heard. And now, what are you waiting for? Arise and be baptized, and wash away your sins, calling on the name of the Lord.

¤ Jesus said, "Rise and stand on your feet; for I have appeared to you for this purpose, to make you a minister and witness both of the things which you have seen and of the things which I will yet reveal to you. I will deliver you from the Jewish people, as well as from the Gentiles, to whom I now send you, to open their eyes, in order to turn them from darkness to light, and from the power of Satan to God, that they may receive forgiveness of sins and an inheritance among those who are sanctified by faith in Me."

¤ All the believers were together and had everything in common. Selling their possessions and goods, they gave to anyone as he/she had need. Every day they continued to meet together. They broke bread in their homes and ate together with glad and sincere hearts, praising God and having favor with all the people. And the Lord added to their number daily those who were being saved.

¤ Since we have been justified through faith, we have peace with God through our Lord Jesus Christ, through whom we have gained access by faith into this grace in which we now stand. And we rejoice in hope... And hope does not disappoint us, because God has poured out His love into our hearts by the Holy Spirit, whom He has given us.

Acts 22:14-16, Acts 26:16-18, Acts 2:44-47, Romans 5:1, 2, 5

March 29th / September 29th

I consider that the sufferings of this present time are not worthy to be compared with the glory which shall be revealed in us.

For the earnest expectation of the creation eagerly waits for the revealing of the sons of God. For the creation was subject to futility, not willingly, but because of Him who subjected it in hope; because the creation itself also will be delivered from the bondage of corruption into the glorious liberty of the children of God. For we know that the whole creation groans and labors with birth pangs together until now.

Not only this, but we also who have the first-fruits of the Spirit, even we ourselves groan within ourselves, eagerly waiting for the adoption, the redemption of our body. For we were saved in this hope, but hope that is seen is not hope; for why does one still hope for what he sees? But if we hope for what we do not see, we eagerly wait for it with perseverance... And the Spirit helps us in our weaknesses... And we know that all things work together for good to those who love God, to those who are called according to His purpose.

Romans 8:18-26, 28

March 30th / September 30th

Just as it is written: "Jacob I loved, but Esau I hated."

What shall we say? Is God unjust? Not at all! For He says to Moses, "I will have mercy on whom I will have mercy, and I will have compassion on whom I will have compassion."

It does not, therefore, depend upon man's desire or effort, but on God's mercy. For the Scripture says to Pharaoh: "I raised you up for this very purpose, that I might display My power in you and that My name might be proclaimed in all the earth." Therefore God has mercy on whom He wants to have mercy, and He hardens whom he wants to harden.

One of you will say to me: "Then why does God still find fault with us? For who resists His will?" But indeed, who are you to reply against God? Will the thing formed say to Him who formed it, "Why have You made me like this?" Does not the potter have the right to make out of the same lump of clay some pottery for noble purposes and some for common use?

What if God, choosing to show His wrath and make His power known, bore with great patience the objects of His wrath prepared for destruction? What if He did this to make the riches of His glory known to the objects of His mercy, whom He prepared in advance for glory—even us, whom He also called, not only from the Jews but also from the Gentiles?

¤ God is not unjust; He will not forget your work and the love you have shown Him as you have helped His people and continue to help them... Continue then to imitate those who through faith and patience inherit what has been promised.

Romans 9:13-24, Hebrews 6:10, 12

113

March 31st

Now faith is being sure of what we hope for and certain of what we can not see.

This is what the ancients were commended for. By faith we understand that the universe was formed at God's command, so that the things which are seen were not made of things which are visible... Therefore, since we are surrounded by such a great cloud of witnesses, let us throw off everything that hinders and the sin that so easily entangles, and let us run with perseverance the race marked out for us.

Let us fix our eyes on Jesus, the author and perfecter of our faith, who for the joy set before Him endured the cross, scorning its shame, and sat down at the right hand of the throne of God. Consider Him who endured such opposition from sinful men, so that you will not grow weary and lose heart.

In your struggle against sin, you have not yet resisted to the point of shedding your blood. And you have forgotten that word of encouragement that addresses you as sons: "My son, do not make light of the Lord's discipline, and do not lose heart when He rebukes you, because the Lord disciplines those whom He loves, and He and punishes everyone He accepts as a son."

Endure hardship as discipline; God is treating you as sons and daughters. For what child is not disciplined by his/her father? If you are not disciplined (and everyone undergoes discipline), then you are illegitimate children and not His true offspring...

Therefore strengthen the hands which hang down, and the feeble knees. Make straight paths for your feet, so that what is lame may not become disabled, but rather be healed. ¤ Be strong and courageous. Do not be afraid or terrified of your ordeals and trials, for the Lord your God goes with you.

May The HoWL of The WOLVES Live Forever, and
Guide All Peoples, of Present and Future.
You Can Feel 'One' Love, from a Pack. p wolf

<<WOLF SPIRIT>>
facebook

Hebrews 11:1-3, Hebrews 12:1-8, 12, 13, Deuteronomy 31:6

115

April 1ˢᵗ
October 1ˢᵗ

And God called the dry land Earth, and the gathering together of the waters He called Seas. And God saw that it was good.

¤ He spreads out the northern skies over empty space; He suspends the earth over nothing. He wraps up the waters in His clouds, yet the clouds do not burst under their weight. He covers the face of the full moon, spreading His clouds over it. He marks out the horizon on the face of the waters for a boundary between light and darkness... And these are but the outer fringe of His works; how faint the whisper we hear of Him! Who then can understand the thunder of His power?

¤ He said to me, "You are My Son, today I have become your Father. Ask of Me, and I will make the nations Your inheritance, the ends of the earth Your possession. You will rule them with an iron scepter, You will dash them to pieces like pottery."

Therefore you kings be wise; be warned, you rulers of the earth. Serve the Lord with fear and rejoice with trembling. Kiss the Son, lest He be angry and you be destroyed in your way, for His wrath can flare up in a moment. Blessed are all who take refuge in Him. ¤ Leave your simple ways and you will live; walk in the way of understanding.

Genesis 1:10, Job 26:7-10, 14, Psalm 2:7-12, Proverbs 9:6

April 2nd / October 2nd

*He found me in a desert
land...*

And in the wasteland, a howling wilderness; He encircled me, He instructed me, He kept me as the apple of His eye. As an eagle stirs up its nest, hovers over its young, spreading out its wings, taking them up, carrying them on its wings, so the Lord alone led me. ¤ He bore me on eagles wings and brought me to Himself. ¤ All the earth is filled with the glory of the Lord.

¤ May my cry come before You, O Lord; give me understanding according to Your word. May my supplication come before You; deliver me according to Your promise. May my lips overflow with praise, for You teach me Your decrees. May my tongue sing of Your word, for all Your commands are righteous. May Your hand be ready to help me, for I have chosen Your precepts.

I long for Your salvation, O Lord, and Your law is my delight. Let me live that I may praise You, and may Your laws sustain me. I have stayed like a lost sheep. Seek Your servant, for I have not forgotten Your commands.

¤ I know that the Lord will maintain the cause of the afflicted, and justice for the poor. Surely the righteous will give thanks to Your name; the upright will dwell in Your presence. ¤ I know that You can do all things, and that no purpose of Yours can be thwarted. ¤ I will bless the Lord who has counseled me; Indeed, my mind instructs me in the night.

*Deuteronomy 32:10-12, Exodus 19:4, Numbers 14:21,
Psalm 119:169-176, Psalm 140:12, 13, Job 42:2, Psalm 15:7*

April 3rd / October 3rd

I speak the truth in Christ.

¤ I want to know Christ and the power of His resurrection and the fellowship of sharing in His sufferings, becoming like Him in His death, and so, somehow, to attain to the resurrection from the dead. Not that I have already obtained all this, or have already been made perfect, but I press on to take hold of that for which Christ Jesus took hold of me.

I do not consider myself yet to have taken hold of it. But one thing I do: Forgetting what is behind and straining toward what is ahead, I press on toward the goal to win the prize for which God has called me heavenward in Christ Jesus. All of us who are mature should take such a view of things. And if on some point you think differently, that too God will make clear to you. Only let us live up to what we have already attained.

¤ And we pray for this in order that you may live a life worthy of the Lord and may please Him in every way; bearing fruit in every good work, growing in the knowledge of God, being strengthened with all power according to His glorious might, so that you may have great endurance and patience and joyful giving of thanks to the Father, who has qualified you to share in the inheritance of the saints in the kingdom of light.

For He has rescued us from the dominion of darkness and translated us into the kingdom of the Son He loves, in whom we have redemption, the forgiveness of sins. ¤ Christ gave Himself for us to redeem us from all wickedness and to purify for Himself a people that are His very own, eager to do what is good.

Romans 9:1, Philippians 3:10-16, Colossians 1:10-14, Titus 2:14

April 4th
October 4th

Be strong in the Lord and in His mighty power.

Put on the full armor of God so that you can take your stand against the devil's schemes. For our struggle is not against flesh and blood, but against the rulers, against the authorities, against the powers of this dark world and against spiritual forces of evil in the heavenly realms.

¤ "They make ready their tongue like a bow, to shoot lies; it is not by truth that they triumph in the land. They go from one sin to another; they do not acknowledge Me," declares the Lord... "They have taught their tongues to lie; they weary themselves with sinning. You live in the midst of deception; in their deceit they refuse to acknowledge Me."

¤ This is what God the Lord says—He who created the heavens and stretched them out, who spread out the earth and all that comes out of it, who gives breath to its people, and life to those who walk on it: "I the Lord, have called you in righteousness; I will take hold of your hand. I will keep you and make you a light for the people, to open eyes that are blind, to free captives from prison and release from the dungeon those who sit in darkness."

¤ Do not gloat over me, my enemy! Though I have fallen, I will rise. Though I sit in darkness, the Lord will be my light.

Ephesians 6:10-12, Jeremiah 9:3, 5, 6, Isaiah 42: 5-7, Micah 7:8

April 5th
October 5th

Enter through the narrow gate...

For wide is the gate and broad is the road that leads to destruction, and many enter through it. But small is the gate and narrow the road that leads to life, and only a few find it.

Watch out for false teachers, who come to you in sheep's clothing, but inwardly they are ferocious wolves. By their fruit you will recognize them. Do people pick grapes from thorn bushes, or figs from thistles? Likewise every good tree bears good fruit, but a bad tree bears bad fruit. A good tree cannot bear bad fruit, and a bad tree cannot bear good fruit. Every tree that does not bear good fruit is cut down and thrown into the fire. Thus, by their fruit you will recognize them.

¤ There were false prophets among the people of old, just as there will be false teachers among you. They will secretly introduce destructive heresies, even denying the sovereign Lord who bought them—bringing swift destruction upon themselves. Many will follow their shameful ways and will bring the way of truth into disrepute. In their greed these teachers will exploit you with stories they have made up. But, their condemnation has long been hanging over them, and their destruction has not been sleeping.

¤ And so, dear friends, do not believe every spirit, but test the spirits to see whether or not they are from God, because many false teachers have gone out into the world.

Matthew 7:13-20, 2nd Peter 2:1-3, 1st John 4:1

April 6th / October 6th

Everyone who believes that Jesus is the Christ is born of God...

And everyone who loves the Father loves His child as well. This is how we know that we love the children of God: by loving God and carrying out His commands. This is love for God: to obey His commands. And His commands are not burdensome, for everyone born of God overcomes the world. This is the victory that has overcome the world, even our faith. Who is it that overcomes the world? Only he/she that believes that Jesus is the Son of God.

¤ Therefore, dear friends, since you already know this, be on your guard so that you may not be carried away by the error of lawless men and fall from your secure position. But grow in the grace and knowledge of our Lord and Savior Jesus Christ. To Him be glory both now and forever.

¤ Who is going to harm you if you are eager to do good? But even if you should suffer for what is right, you are blessed. Do not fear what they fear; do not be frightened. But in your hearts set apart Christ as Lord. Always be prepared to give an answer to everyone who asks you to give the reason for the hope that you have.

¤ Who is wise and understanding among you? Let he/she show it by their good life; by deeds done in the humility that comes from wisdom. ¤ See to it that none of you have a sinful, unbelieving heart that turns away from the living God. Instead, encourage one another daily, as long as it is called today.

1st John 5:1-5, 2nd Peter 3:17, 18, 1st Peter 3:13-15, James 3:13, Hebrews 3:12, 13

April 7th / October 7th

The body is a unit, though it is made up of many parts.

 And though all its parts are many, they form one body. So it is with Christ. For we were all baptized by one Spirit into one body—whether Jews or Greeks, slave or free—and we were all given the one Spirit to drink...

If the foot should say, "Because I am not a hand, I do not belong to the body," it would not for that reason cease to be a part of the body. And if the ear should say, "Because I am not an eye, I do not belong to the body," it would not for that reason cease to be a part of the body. If the whole body were an eye, where would the sense of hearing be? If the whole body were an ear, where would the sense of smell be?

But in fact God has arranged the parts in the body, every one of them, just as He wanted them to be. If they were all one part, where would the body be? As it is, there are many parts, but one body. The eye cannot say to the hand, "I don't need you!" And the head cannot say to the feet, "I don't need you!" On the contrary, those parts of the body that seem to be weaker are necessary, and the parts that we think are less honorable are treated with greater honor. And the parts of the body that are unrepresentable are treated with special modesty, while our presentable parts need no special treatment.

But God has combined the members of the body and has given greater honor to the parts that lacked it, so that there should be no division in the body, but that its parts should have equal concern for each other. If one part is honored, every part rejoices with it. Now, you are the body of Christ, and each one of you is a part of it. ¤ For as many of you who were baptized into Christ have put on Christ.

1st Corinthians 12:12, 13, 15-27, Galatians 3:27

122

April 8th / October 8th

Hear my cry, O God; listen to my prayer.

From the ends of the earth I call to You, I call as my heart grows faint; lead me to the rock that is higher than I. For You have been my refuge, a strong tower against the foe.

¤ May God be gracious to us and bless us and make His face shine upon us, so that Your ways may be known on earth, Your salvation among the nations. May the peoples praise You, O God; may all the peoples praise You. May the nations be glad and sing for joy, for You rule the peoples justly and guide the nations of the earth.

¤ He is the rock. His works are perfect, and all His ways are just. A faithful God who does no wrong, upright and just is He. They have acted corruptly toward Him; to their shame they are no longer His children, but a warped and crooked generation. Is this the way that you repay the Lord, O foolish and unwise people? Is He not your Father, your creator, who made you and formed you?

¤ I love You, O Lord, my strength. The Lord is my rock, my fortress and my deliverer; My God is my rock, in whom I take refuge. He is my shield and the horn of my salvation, my stronghold. I call to the Lord, who is worthy of praise, and I am saved from my enemies... He brought me out into a spacious place; He rescued me because He delighted in me.

Psalm 61:1, 2, Psalm 68:1-4, Deuteronomy 32:4-6, Psalm 18:1-3, 19

April 9th / October 9th

Blessed are those whose way is blameless, who walk in the law of the Lord.

How blessed are those who observe His testimonies, who seek Him with all their heart. They also do no unrighteousness; they walk in His ways. You have ordained Your precepts, that we should keep them diligently. Oh that my ways may be established to keep Your statutes! Then I shall not be ashamed when I look upon all Your commandments. I shall give thanks to You with uprightness of heart, when I learn of Your righteous judgments. I shall keep Your statutes; do not forsake me utterly!

How can a young man keep His way pure? By keeping it according to Your word. With all my heart I have sought You; do not let me wander from Your commandments. Your word I have treasured in my heart, that I might not sin against You. Blessed are You, O Lord; teach me Your statutes. With my lips I have told of all the ordinances of Your mouth. I have rejoiced in the way of Your testimonies, as much as in all the riches. I will meditate on Your precepts and regard Your ways. I shall delight in Your statutes, I shall not forget Your word.

Deal bountifully with Your servant, that I may live and keep Your word. Open my eyes that I may behold wonderful things from Your law. I am a stranger in the earth; do not hide your commandments from me. My soul is crushed with longing after Your ordinances at all times. You rebuke the arrogant, the cursed, who wander from Your commandments. Take away reproach and contempt from me, for I observe Your testimonies. Even though princes sit and talk against me, Your servant meditates on Your statutes. Your testimonies also are my delight; they are my counselors.

Psalm 119:1-24

April 10th / October 10th

My soul cleaves to the dust; revive me according to Your word.

I have told of my ways, and You have answered me; teach me your statutes. Make me understand the way of Your precepts, so that I will meditate on Your wonders. My soul weeps because of grief; strengthen me according to Your word. Remove the false way from me, and graciously grant me Your law. I have chosen the faithful way; I have placed Your ordinances before me. I cling to Your testimonies; O Lord, do not put me to shame! I shall run the way of Your commandments, For You will enlarge my heart.

Teach me, O Lord, the way of Your statutes, and I shall observe it to the end. Give me understanding, that I may observe Your law and keep it with all my heart. Make me walk in the path of Your commandments, for I delight in it. Incline my heart to Your testimonies and not to dishonest gain. Turn away my eyes from looking at vanity, and revive me in Your ways. Establish Your word to Your servant, as that which produces reverence for you. Turn away my reproach which I dread, for Your ordinances are good. Behold, I long for Your precepts; revive me through Your righteousness.

May Your loving-kindness also come to me, O Lord, Your salvation according to Your word; so that I will have an answer to him who reproaches me, for I trust in Your word. And do not take the word of truth utterly out of my mouth, for I wait for Your ordinances. So I will keep your law continually, forever and ever. And I will walk at liberty, for I seek Your precepts. I will also speak of your testimonies before kings and shall not be ashamed. I shall delight in Your commandments, which I love. And I shall lift up my hands to Your commandments, Which I love; and I will meditate on Your statutes.

Psalm 119:25-48

127

April 11th / October 11th

Remember the word to Your servant, in which You have made me hope.

This is my comfort in my affliction, that Your word has revived me. The arrogant utterly deride me, yet I do not turn aside from Your law. I have remembered Your ordinances from of old, O Lord, and comfort myself. Burning indignation has seized me because of the wicked, who forsake Your law. Your statutes are my songs in the house of my pilgrimage. O Lord, I remember Your name in the night, and keep Your law. This has become mine, that I observe Your precepts.

The Lord is my portion; I have promised to keep Your words. I sought Your favor with all my heart; be gracious to me according to Your word. I considered my ways and turned my feet to Your testimonies. I hastened and did not delay to keep Your commandments. The cords of the wicked have encircled me, but I have not forgotten Your law. At midnight I shall rise to give thanks to You because of Your righteous ordinances. I am a companion of all those who fear You, and of those who keep Your precepts. The earth is full of Your loving-kindness, O Lord; teach me Your statutes.

You have dealt well with Your servant, O Lord, according to Your word. Teach me good discernment and knowledge, for I believe in Your commandments. Before I was afflicted I went astray, but now I keep Your word. You are good and do good; teach me Your statutes. The arrogant have forged a lie against me; with all my heart I will observe Your precepts. Their heart is covered with fat, but I delight in Your law. It is good for me that I was afflicted, that I may learn Your statutes. The law of Your mouth is better to me than thousands of gold and silver pieces.

Psalm 119:49-72

April 12th / October 12th

Your hands have made me and fashioned me.

Give me understanding that I may learn Your commandments. May those who fear You see me and be glad, because I wait for Your word. I know, O Lord, that Your judgments are righteous, and that in faithfulness You have afflicted me. O may Your loving-kindness comfort me, according to Your word to Your servant. May Your compassion come to me that I may live, for Your law is my delight. May the arrogant be ashamed, for they subvert me with a lie; but I shall meditate on Your precepts. May those who fear You turn to me, even those who know Your testimonies. May my heart be blameless in Your statutes, so that I will not be ashamed.

My soul languishes for Your salvation; I wait for Your word. My eyes fail with longing for Your word, while I say, "When will You comfort me?" Though I have become like a wineskin in the smoke, I do not forget Your statutes. How many are the days of Your servant? When will You execute judgment on those who persecute me? The arrogant have dug pits for me, men who are not in accord with Your law. All Your commandments are faithful; they have persecuted me with a lie; help me! They almost destroyed me on earth, but as for me, I did not forsake Your precepts. Revive me according to Your loving-kindness, so that I may keep the testimony of Your mouth.

Forever, O Lord, Your word is settled in heaven. Your faithfulness continues throughout all generations; You established the earth, and it stands. They stand this day according to Your ordinances, for all things are Your servants. If Your law had not been my delight, then I would have perished in my affliction. I will never forget Your precepts, for by them You have revived me.

I am Yours; save me; for I have sought Your precepts. The wicked wait for me to destroy me; I shall diligently consider Your testimonies. I have seen the consummation of all perfection; but Your commandment is exceedingly broad.

Psalm 119:73-96

April 13th / October 13th

O how I love Your law! It is my meditation all the day.

Your commandments make me wiser than my enemies, for they are ever mine. I have more insight than all my teachers, for Your testimonies are my meditation. I understand more than the aged, because I have observed Your precepts. I have restrained my feet from every evil way, that I may keep Your word. I have not turned aside from Your ordinances, for You yourself have taught me. How sweet are Your words to my taste! Yes sweeter than honey to my mouth! From Your precepts I get understanding; therefore I hate every false way.

Your word is a lamp to my feet and a light to my path. I have sworn and I will confirm it, that I will keep your righteous ordinances. I am exceedingly afflicted; revive me, O Lord, according to Your word. O accept the freewill offerings of my mouth, O Lord, and teach me Your ordinances. My life is continually in my hand, yet I do not forget Your law. The wicked have laid a snare for me, yet I have not gone astray from Your precepts. I have inherited Your testimonies forever, for they are the joy of my heart. I have inclined my heart to perform Your statutes forever, even to the end.

I hate those who are double-minded, but I love Your law. You are my hiding place and my shield; I wait for Your word. Depart from me, evildoers, that I may observe the commandments of my God. Sustain me according to Your word, that I may live; and do not let me be ashamed of my hope. Uphold me that I may be safe, that I may have regard for Your statutes continually. You have rejected all those who wander from Your statutes, for their deceitfulness is useless. You have removed all the wicked of the earth like dross; therefore I love Your testimonies. My flesh trembles for fear of You, and I am afraid of Your judgments.

Psalm 119:97-120

April 14th / October 14th

I have done justice and righteousness; do not leave me to my oppressors.

Be surety for your servant for good; do not let the arrogant oppress me. My eyes fail with longing for Your salvation and for Your righteous word. Deal with Your servant according to Your loving-kindness and teach me Your statutes. I am Your servant; give me understanding, that I may know Your testimonies. It is time for the Lord to act, for they have broken Your law. Therefore I love Your commandments above gold, yes, above fine gold. Therefore I esteem right all Your precepts concerning everything, and I hate every false way.

Your testimonies are wonderful; therefore my soul observes them. The unfolding of Your word gives light; gives understanding to the simple. I opened my mouth wide and panted, for I longed for Your commandments. Turn to me and be gracious to me, as Your custom is with those who love Your name. Establish my footsteps in Your word, and do not let iniquity have dominion over me. Redeem me from the oppression of man, that I may keep Your precepts. Make Your face shine upon Your servant, and teach me Your statutes. My eyes shed streams of water, because they do not keep Your law.

Righteous are You, O Lord, and upright are Your judgments. You have commanded Your testimonies in righteousness and exceeding faithfulness. My zeal has consumed me, because my adversaries have forgotten Your words. Your word is very pure, therefore Your servant loves it. I am small and despised, yet I do not forget Your precepts. Your righteousness is an everlasting righteousness, and Your law is truth.

Psalm 119:121-142

April 15th / October 15th

Trouble and anguish have come upon me, yet Your commandments are my delight.

Your testimonies are righteous forever; give me understanding that I may live. I cried with all my heart; answer me, O Lord! I will observe Your statutes. I cried to You; save me and I shall keep Your testimonies. I rise before dawn and cry for help; I wait for Your words. My eyes anticipate the night watches, that I may meditate on Your word. Hear my voice according to Your loving-kindness; revive me, O Lord, according to Your ordinances. Those who follow after wickedness draw near; they are far from Your law. You are near, O Lord, and all of Your commandments are truth. Of old I have known from Your testimonies that You have founded them forever.

Look upon my affliction and rescue me, for I do not forget Your law. Plead my cause and redeem me; revive me according to Your word. Salvation is far from the wicked, for they do not seek Your statutes. Great are Your mercies, O Lord; revive me according to Your ordinances. Many are my persecutors and my adversaries, yet I do not turn aside from Your testimonies. I behold the treacherous and loathe them, because they do not keep Your word. Consider how I love Your precepts; revive me, O Lord, according to Your loving-kindness. The sum of Your word is truth, and every one of Your righteous ordinances is everlasting.

Princes persecute me without cause, but my heart stands in awe of Your words. I rejoice at Your word, as one who finds great treasure. I hate and despise falsehood, but I love Your law.

Psalm 119:143-163

135

April 16th / October 16th

Seven times a day I praise You, because of Your righteous ordinances.

Those who love Your law have great peace, and nothing causes them to stumble. I hope for Your salvation, O Lord, and do Your commandments. My soul keeps Your testimonies, and I love them exceedingly. I keep Your precepts and testimonies, for all my ways are before You.

Let my cry come before You, O Lord; give me understanding according to Your word. Let my supplication come before You; deliver me according to Your word. Let my lips utter praise, for You teach me Your statutes. Let my tongue sing of Your word, for all of Your commandments are righteousness. Let Your hand be ready to help me, for I have chosen Your precepts. I long for Your salvation, O Lord, and Your law is my delight.

Let my soul live that it may praise You, and let Your ordinances help me. I have gone astray like a lost sheep; seek Your servant, for I do not forget Your commandments.

¤ To You I lift of my eyes, O You who are enthroned in the heavens! Behold, as the eyes of servants look to their master, as the eyes of a maid to her mistress, so our eyes look to the Lord our God, until He is gracious to us. ¤ Those who trust in the Lord are as Mount Zion, which cannot be moved but abides forever. ¤ Trust in the Lord with all of your heart and do not lean on your own understanding.

Psalm 119:164-176, Psalm 123:1, 2, Psalm 125:1, Proverbs 3:5

April 17th / October 17th

For though we walk in the flesh, we do not war according to the flesh.

For the weapons of our warfare are not carnal but mighty in God for pulling down strongholds, casting down arguments and every high thing that exalts itself against the knowledge of God, and bringing every thought into captivity to the obedience of Christ... ¤ Therefore we are debtors—not to the flesh, to live according to the flesh. For if you live according to the flesh you will die; but if by the Spirit you put to death the deeds of the body, you will live. For as many as are led by the Spirit of God, these are the sons of God.

¤ I say then: Walk in the Spirit, and you shall not fulfill the lust of the flesh. For the flesh lusts against the Spirit, and the Spirit against the flesh; and these are contrary to one another, so that you do not do the things that you wish. But if you are led by the Spirit, you are not under the law.

Now the works of the flesh are evident, which are: adultery, fornication, uncleanness, lewdness, idolatry, sorcery, hatred, contentions, jealousies, outbursts of wrath, selfish ambitions, dissensions, heresies, envy, murders, drunkenness, revelries, and the like; of which I tell you beforehand, just as I also told you in times past, that those who practice such things will not inherit the kingdom of God.

But the fruit of the Spirit is love, joy, peace, long-suffering (patience), kindness, goodness, faithfulness, gentleness, and self-control. Against such there is no law... If we live in the Spirit, let us also walk in the Spirit.

2nd Corinthians 10:3-5, Romans 8:12-14, 5:16-23, 25

Galatians

137

April 18th / October 18th

*If a man sins against another man,
God may mediate for him; but if a
man sins against the Lord, who will
intercede for him?*

¤ If anyone does sin, we have an Advocate with the Father
—Jesus Christ the righteous. And He himself is the propitiation
for our sins, and not for ours only, but also for the sins of the
whole world. ¤ Though He was a Son, He learned obedience by
the things which He suffered. And having been perfected, He
became the Author of eternal salvation to all who obey Him.

¤ Therefore, let us lay aside every weight, and the sin which
so easily ensnares us, and let us run with endurance the race that
is set before us, looking unto Jesus, the author and finisher of
our faith, who for the joy that was set before Him endured the
cross, despising the shame, and has sat down at the right hand of
God. For consider Him who endured such hostility from sinners
against Himself, lest you become weary and discouraged in your
souls.

For you have not yet resisted to the point of shedding blood
in your struggle against sin. And you have forgotten that word of
encouragement which addresses you as sons: "My son, do not
make light of the Lord's discipline, and do not lose heart when
He rebukes you, because the Lord disciplines those whom He
loves, and He punishes everyone He accepts as a son."

Endure hardship as discipline; God is treating you as sons.
For what son is not disciplined by his father? ...No discipline
seems pleasant at the time, but painful. Later on, however, it
produces a harvest of righteousness and peace for those who
have been trained by it.

1st Samuel 2:25, 1st John 2:1, 2, Hebrews 5:8, 9, Hebrews 12:1-7, 11

April 19ᵗʰ / October 19ᵗʰ

We know that all things work together for good to those who love God, to those who are called according to His purpose.

¤ For His eyes are upon the ways of a man, and He sees all of his steps. There is no dark place, no deep shadow, where evildoers can hide. God has no need to examine men further, that they should come before Him for judgment. Without inquiry He shatters the mighty and sets up others in their place. Because He takes note of their deeds, He overthrows them in the night and they are crushed.

He punishes them for their wickedness where everyone can see them, because they turned from following Him and had no regard for any of His ways. They caused the cry of the poor to come before Him, so that He heard the cry of the needy. But if He remains silent, who can condemn Him? If He hides His face, who can see Him? Yet, He is over man and nation alike, to keep godless men from ruling, from laying snares for the people.

¤ Trust in the Lord and do good; dwell in the land and enjoy safe pasture. Delight yourself in the Lord and He will give you the desires of your heart. Commit your way to the Lord; trust in Him and He will do this: He will make your righteousness shine like the dawn, the justice of your cause like the noonday sun. Be still before the Lord and wait patiently for Him; do not fret when men succeed in their ways, when they carry out their wicked schemes.

¤ The fear of the Lord is the beginning of knowledge, but fools despise wisdom and discipline.

Romans 8:28, Job 34:21-30, Psalm 37:3-7, Proverbs 1:7

April 20th
October 20th

"Take courage and work," declares the Lord, "for I am with you."

¤ I am the vine, you are the branches. He who abides in Me and I in him, he bears much fruit, for apart from Me you can do nothing... You did not choose Me, but I chose you and appointed you that you would go and bear fruit, and that your fruit would remain, so that whatever you ask of the Father in My name, He may give to you.

¤ Let your hands be strong. ¤ Strengthen the weak hands, and make firm the feeble knees. Say to those who are of fearful heart, "Take courage and fear not.".....You will find gladness and joy; and sorrow and sighing shall flee away.

¤ What then shall we say to these things? If God is for us, who can be against us? ...In all things we overwhelmingly conquer through Him who loved us. For I am convinced that neither death, nor life, neither angels nor demons, neither the present nor the future, nor any powers, neither height nor depth, nor anything else in all creation, will be able to separate us from the love of God that is in Christ Jesus our Lord.

¤ I would have despaired unless I had believed that I would see the goodness of the Lord in the land of the living. Wait for the Lord; be strong and let your heart take courage; Yes, wait for the Lord. ¤ The Lord your God is the one who goes with you. He will not fail you or forsake you.

Haggai 2:4, John 15:5, 16, Zechariah 8:9, Isaiah 35:3, 4, 10,
Romans 8:31, 37-39, Psalm 27:13, 14, Deuteronomy 31:6

April 21st
October 21st

At this my heart pounds and leaps from its place.

Listen to the roar of His voice, to the rumbling that comes from His mouth. He unleashes His lightning beneath the whole heaven and sends it to the ends of the earth. After that comes the sound of His roar; He thunders with His majestic voice. When His voice resounds, He holds nothing back.

God's voice thunders in marvelous ways; He does great things beyond our understanding. He says to the snow, 'Fall on the earth,' and to the rain shower, 'Be a mighty downpour.' So that all men He has made know His work, He stops every man from his labor. The animals take cover; they remain in their dens. The tempest comes out from its chamber, the cold from the driving winds.

The breath of God produces ice, and the broad waters become frozen. He loads the clouds with moisture; He scatters His lightning through them. At His direction they swirl around over the face of the whole earth to do whatever He commands them. He brings the clouds to punish men, or to water His earth and show His love... Therefore men revere Him, for does He not have regard for all the wise in heart?

¤ O Lord my God, I take refuge in You; save and deliver me from all who pursue me, or they will tear me like a lion and rip me to pieces with no one to rescue me... O righteous God, who searches minds and hearts, bring an end to the violence of the wicked and make the righteous secure.

Job 37:1-13, 24, Psalm 7:1, 2, 9

141

April 22ⁿᵈ / October 22ⁿᵈ

Jesus said, "The thief comes only to steal and kill and destroy; I came that people may have life, and have it abundantly."

I am the good shepherd; the good shepherd lays down His life for the sheep. He who is a hired hand, and not a shepherd, who is not the owner of the sheep, sees the wolf coming, and leaves the sheep and flees. The wolf then snatches all the sheep and scatters them. The hired man flees because he is not concerned about the sheep.

¤ Now the pharisees and their scribes began grumbling at Jesus' disciples, saying, "Why do you eat and drink with the tax collectors and sinners?" And Jesus answered and said to them, "It is not those who are well who need a physician, but those who are sick. I have not come to call the righteous, but sinners to repentance."

¤ "Not everyone who says to Me, 'Lord, Lord,' will enter the kingdom of heaven, but it is he that does the will of My Father in heaven who will enter... Everyone who hears these words of Mine and does not act on them will be like a foolish man who built his house on the sand. The rain fell, and the floods came, and the winds blew and slammed against the house; and it fell—and great was its fall!"

¤ All sins shall be forgiven the sons of men, and whatever blasphemies they utter; but whoever blasphemies (speaks impiously or irreverently) against the Holy Spirit never has forgiveness, but is guilty of eternal sin.

John 10:10-13, Luke 5:30-32, Matthew 7:21, 26, 27, Mark 3:28, 29

April 23rd / October 23rd

Now the whole world had one language and a common speech.

As men moved eastward, they found a plain in Shinar and settled there... Then they said, "Come, let us build ourselves a city, with a tower that reaches to the heavens, so that we may make a name for ourselves and not be scattered over the face of the whole earth."

But the Lord came down to see the city and the tower that the men were building. The Lord then said, "If as one people speaking one language they have begun to do this, then nothing they plan to do will be impossible for them. Come, let us go down and confuse their language⁵ so that they will not understand each other."

So the Lord scattered them from there over all the earth, and they stopped building the city. That is why it is called Babel to this day—because there the Lord confused the language of all the people. From there the Lord scattered them over the face of the whole earth.

¤ And Job said to the Lord, "I know that You can do all things; no plan of Yours can be thwarted... My ears had heard of You, but now my eyes have seen You. Therefore I despise myself, and repent in dust and ashes."

¤ Oh, the depth of the riches of the wisdom and knowledge of God! How unsearchable are His judgments, and His paths beyond tracing out! Who has known the mind of the Lord? Or who has been His counselor? ...From Him and through Him are all things.

Genesis 11:1, 2, 4-9, Job 42:2, 5, 6, Romans 11:33, 34, 36

143

April 24th / October 24th

Be careful that you do not forget the Lord your God.

¤ Do not let the word of the Lord depart from your mouth; meditate on it day and night, so that you may be careful to do everything written in it. Then you will be prosperous and successful. "Have I not commanded you? Be strong and courageous. Do not be terrified; do not be discouraged, for the Lord your God will be with you wherever you go."

¤ Do not learn the ways of the nations or be terrified by signs in the sky, though the nations are terrified by them. For the customs of the people are worthless. ¤ Do not conform any longer to the pattern of this world, but be transformed by the renewing of your mind. Then you will be able to test and approve what God's will is—His good pleasing and perfect will.

¤ Prepare your minds for action, keep sober in spirit, fix your hope completely on the grace to be brought to you at the revelation of Jesus Christ. As obedient children, do not be conformed to the former lusts which were yours in ignorance, but like the Holy One who called you, be holy yourselves also in all of your behavior; because it is written, "You shall be holy, for I am holy."

¤ Who among you is wise and understanding? Let him/her show you by their good life, by deeds done in the humility that comes from wisdom. But if you harbor bitter envy and selfish ambition in your hearts, do not boast about it or deny the truth. Such "wisdom" does not come down from heaven, but is earthly, nonspiritual, and of the devil.

*Deuteronomy 8:11, Joshua 1:8, 9, Jeremiah 10:2, 3, Romans 12:2,
1st Peter 1:13-16, James 3:13-15*

April 25th / October 25th

Oh Lord, You have searched me and known me.

You know when I sit down and when I rise up; You understand my thoughts from afar. You scrutinize my path and my lying down, and are intimately acquainted with all of my ways. Even before there is a word on my tongue, behold, O Lord, You know it all. You hem me in—behind and before, and have laid Your hand upon me. Such knowledge is too wonderful for me; It is too high, I can not attain to it.

Where can I go from Your Spirit? Or where can I flee from Your presence? If I ascend to heaven, You are there; If I make my bed in the depths of the earth, You are there. If I rise on the wings of the dawn, if I dwell in the remotest part of the sea, even there Your hand will guide me, Your right hand will lay hold of me. If I say, "Surely the darkness will overwhelm me, and the light become night around me," yet even the darkness will not be dark to You, and the night is as bright as the day. Darkness and light are both alike to You.

For You created my inmost being; You wove me together in my mother's womb. I praise You because I am fearfully and wonderfully made.[6] Wonderful are Your works, and my soul knows it very well. My frame was not hidden from You when I was made in the secret place, skilfully woven together in the depths of the earth. Your eyes saw my unformed body, and all the days ordained for me were written in Your book before one of them came to be.

How precious also are Your thoughts to me, O God! How vast is the sum of them! If I were to count them, they would outnumber the grains of sand. And when I awake, I am still with You.

Psalm 139:1-18

April 26th / October 26th

To You I will call, O Lord my Rock.

Do not turn a deaf ear to me. For if You remain silent, I will be like those who have gone down to the pit. Hear my cry for mercy as I call to You for help, as I lift up my hands toward Your Most Holy Place.

Do not drag me away with the wicked, with those who do evil, who speak cordially with their neighbors, but harbor malice in their hearts. Repay them for their deeds and for their evil work; repay them for what their hands have done and bring back upon them what they deserve. Since they show no regard for the works of the Lord and what His hands have done, He will tear them down and never build them up again.

Praise be to the Lord, for He has heard my cry for mercy. The Lord is my strength and my shield; my heart trusts in Him and I am helped. My heart leaps for joy and I will give thanks to Him in song. The Lord is the strength of His people, a fortress of salvation for His anointed ones. Save Your people and bless Your inheritance; be their Shepherd and carry them forever.

¤ I will exalt You, O Lord, for You lifted me out of the depths and did not let my enemies gloat over me. O Lord my God, I called to You for help and You healed me. O Lord, You brought me up from the grave; You spared me from going down into the pit.

Sing to the Lord, you saints of His; praise His holy name. For His anger lasts only a moment, but His favor lasts a lifetime; weeping may remain for a night, but rejoicing comes in the morning.

When I felt secure, I said, "I will never be shaken." O Lord, when You favored me, You made my mountain stand firm; but

146

when You hid Your face, I was dismayed. To You, O Lord, I called; to the Lord I cried for mercy: "What gain is there in my destruction, in my going down into the pit? Will the dust praise You? Will it proclaim Your faithfulness? Hear, O Lord, and be merciful to me; O Lord, be my help."

You turned my wailing into dancing; You removed my sackcloth and clothed me with joy, that my heart may sing to You and not be silent. O Lord my God, I will give thanks to You forever.

Psalm 28, Psalm 30

147

April 27th / October 27th

In You, O Lord, I have taken refuge.

Let me never be put to shame; deliver me in Your righteousness. Turn Your ear to me, come quickly to my rescue; be my rock of strength, a strong fortress to save me. Since You are my rock and my fortress, for the sake of Your name lead and guide me. Free me from the trap that is set for me, for You are my refuge. Into Your hands I commit my spirit; redeem me, O Lord, the God of truth.

¤ When I kept silent, my bones wasted away through my groaning all day long. For day and night Your hand was heavy upon me; my strength was sapped as in the heat of summer. Then I acknowledged my sin to You and did not cover up my iniquity. I said, "I will confess my transgressions to the Lord— and You forgave the guilt of my sin."

¤ The angel of the Lord encamps around those who fear Him, and He delivers them. Fear the Lord, you His saints, for those who fear Him lack nothing. The lions may grow weak and hungry, but those who seek the Lord lack no good thing.

¤ Do not fret because of evil men or be envious of those who do wrong; for like the grass they will soon wither, like green plants they will soon die away. Trust in the Lord and do good; dwell in the land and enjoy safe pasture. Delight yourself in the Lord and He will give you the desires of your heart.

Psalm 31:1-5, Psalm 32:3-5, Psalm 34:7-10, Psalm 37:1-4

April 28th / October 28th

*I waited patiently for the
Lord; He turned to me
and heard my cry.*

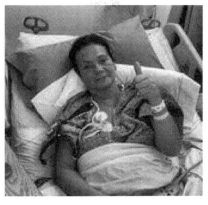

He lifted me out of the
slimy pit, out of the mud and
mire; He set my feet on a
rock and gave me a firm
place to stand. He put a new
song in my mouth, a hymn of praise to our God. Many will see
and fear and put their trust in the Lord.

Blessed is the man who makes the Lord his trust, who does
not look to the proud, to those who turn aside to false gods.
Many, O Lord my God, are the wonders You have done. The
things You planned for us no one can recount to You; were I to
speak of them, they would be too many to declare.

¤ Blessed is he/she who has regard for the weak; the Lord
delivers him/her in times of trouble. The Lord will protect
him/her and preserve their life; He will bless him/her in the land
and not surrender him/her to the desires of their foes. The Lord
will sustain him/her on their sickbed and restore them from their
bed of illness.

¤ God is our refuge and strength, an ever-present help in
time of trouble. Therefore we will not fear, though the earth give
way and the mountains fall into the heart of the sea, though its
waters roar and foam and the mountains quake with their
surging... The Lord Almighty is with us. ¤ God is the King of all
the earth; sing to Him a psalm of praise. ¤ Why should I fear
when evil days come?

Psalm 40:1-5, Psalm 41:1-3, Psalm 46:1-3, 7, Psalm 47:7, Psalm 49:5

April 29th / October 29th

Have mercy on me, O God, according to Your unfailing love.

According to the greatness of Your compassion blot out my transgressions. Wash me thoroughly from my iniquity and cleanse me from my sin. For I know my transgressions, and my sin is ever before me. Against You, You only, I have sinned and done what is evil in Your sight, so that You are justified when You speak, and blameless when You judge.

Truly I was sinful at birth, sinful from the time my mother conceived me. Surely You desire truth in the innermost being, and You will teach me to know wisdom in the inmost place. Cleanse me with hyssop, and I will be clean; wash me, and I will be whiter than snow. Let me hear joy and gladness; let the bones which You have crushed rejoice. Hide Your face from my sins and blot out all of my iniquity.

Create in me a clean heart, O God, and renew a steadfast spirit within me. Do not cast me from Your presence or take Your Holy Spirit from me. Restore me to the joy of Your salvation and grant me a willing spirit to sustain me. Then I will teach transgressors Your ways, and sinners will be converted to You. Save me from blood-guilt, O God, the God who saves me, and my tongue will sing of Your righteousness.

O Lord, open my lips, and my mouth will declare Your praise. You do not delight in sacrifice, or I would bring it; You do not take pleasure in burnt offerings. The sacrifices of God are a broken spirit; a broken spirit and a contrite heart, O God, You will not despise.

Psalm 51

April 30th / October 30th

O God, You are my God, earnestly I seek You.

My soul thirsts for You, my body longs for You, in a dry and weary land where there is no water... Because Your love is greater than life, my lips will glorify You. I will praise You as long as I live, and in Your name I will lift up my hands. My soul will be satisfied as with the richest of foods; with singing lips my mouth will praise You.

On my bed I remember You; I think of You through the watches of the night. Because You are my help, I sing in the shadow of Your wings. My soul clings to You; Your right hand upholds me. ¤ In You, O Lord, I have taken refuge; let me never be put to shame. Rescue me and deliver me in Your righteousness; turn Your ear to me and save me.

Be my rock of refuge, to which I can always go; give the command to save me, for You are my rock and my fortress. Deliver me, O God, from the hand of the wicked, from the grasp of evil and cruel men. For You have been my hope, O Sovereign Lord, my confidence since my youth.

From birth I have relied on You; You brought me forth from my mother's womb. I will ever praise You... Do not cast me away when I am old; do not forsake me when my strength is gone... Since my youth, O God, You have taught me, and to this day I declare Your marvelous deeds...

Though You have made me see troubles, many and bitter, You will restore my life again; from the depths of the earth You will again bring me up.

Psalm 63:1, 3-8, Psalm 71:1-6, 9, 17, 20

151

October 31ˢᵗ

Be careful that you do not fail to forget the Lord your God, failing to observe His commands, His laws, and His decrees.

¤ Now on His way to Jerusalem, Jesus traveled along the border between Samaria and Galilee. As He was going into a village, ten men who had leprosy met Him. They stood at a distance and called out in a loud voice, "Jesus, Master, have mercy on us!"

When He saw them, He said to them, "Go and show yourselves to the priests." And so it was that as they went, they were cleansed. One of them, when he saw that he had been healed, came back, glorifying God in a loud voice. He then threw himself at Jesus' feet, face down in the dust, and thanked Him—and he was a Samaritan.

Jesus asked him, "Were not all ten cleansed? Where are the other nine? Was no one found to return and give glory to God except this foreigner?" He then said to the man, "Rise and go your way; your faith has made you well."

¤ It is the blessing of the Lord that makes one rich, and He adds no sorrow to it. ¤ Bless the Lord, O my soul, and forget none of His benefits; who pardons all of your iniquities, who heals all of your diseases; who redeems your life from the pit, who crowns you with loving-kindness and compassion; who satisfies your years with good things, so that your youth is renewed like the eagle.

¤ "Now consider this, you who forget God, or I will tear you in pieces, and there will be none to deliver: Whoever offers thanksgiving honors Me; and to him/her who orders their conduct aright, I shall show the salvation of God."

Deuteronomy 8:11, Luke 17:11-19, Proverbs 10:22, Psalm 103:2-5, Psalm 50:22, 23

May 1ˢᵗ / November 1ˢᵗ

Let your gentle spirit be known to all. The Lord is near.

¤ For the Lord Himself will descend from heaven with a shout, with the voice of the archangel and with the trumpet of God, and the dead in Christ will rise first. Then we who are alive and remain will be caught up together with them in the clouds to meet the Lord in the air, and so we shall always be with the Lord. Therefore comfort one another with these words.

¤ Now as to the times and dates we do not need to write to you, for you know very well that the day of the Lord will come like a thief in the night. While people are saying, "Peace and safety," destruction will suddenly come upon them, as labor pains on a pregnant woman, and they will not escape. But you are not in darkness that this day should surprise you like a thief.

You are all the children of light and of the day. We do not belong to the night or to the darkness. So then, let us not be like others, who are asleep, but let us be alert and self-controlled... For God did not appoint us to suffer wrath, but to receive salvation through our Lord Jesus Christ.

¤ Listen, I tell you a mystery... We will all be changed—in a flash, in the twinkling of an eye, at the last trumpet. For the trumpet will sound, the dead will be raised imperishable, and we will be changed. For the perishable must clothe itself with the imperishable, and the mortal with immorality.

Philippians4:5, 1ˢᵗ Thessalonians 4:16-18, 1ˢᵗ Thessalonians 5:1-6, 9, 1ˢᵗ Corinthians 15:52, 53

May 2nd / November 2nd

In the past God spoke to our forefathers through the prophets many times, and in various ways, but in these last days He has spoken to us by His Son.

The Son has been appointed heir of all things, and it was through Him that the universe was made. The Son is the radiance of God's glory and the exact representation of His being, sustaining all things by the power of His word. After Jesus had provided purification for sins, He sat down at the right hand of the Majesty in heaven.

So, He has become much superior to the angels as the name He has inherited is superior to theirs... To which of the angels did God ever say, "Sit at My right hand until I make Your enemies a footstool for Your feet"? Are not all angels ministering spirits sent to serve those who will inherit salvation?

¤ Bless the Lord, you His angels, mighty in strength, who perform His word, obeying the voice of His word! ¤ The angel of the Lord encamps all around those who fear Him, and delivers them. ¤ He shall give His angels charge over you, to keep you in all your ways. In their hands they shall bear you up, lest you dash your foot against a stone.

¤ Jesus came from Nazareth in Galilee and was baptized by John in the Jordan. Immediately coming up out of the water, He saw the heavens opening and the Spirit like a dove descending upon Him; and a voice came out of the heavens: "You are My beloved Son; in You I am well pleased." Immediately the Spirit impelled Him to go out into the wilderness. And He was in the wilderness forty days being tempted by Satan; and He was with the wild animals, and angels were attending to Him.

Hebrews 1;1-4, 13, 14, Psalm 103:20, Psalm 34:7, Psalm 91:11, 12, Mark 1:9-13

May 3rd / November 3rd

The angel of the Lord came and sat down under the oak in Ophrah...

Gideon was threshing wheat in a wine press to keep it from the Midianites. When the angel of the Lord appeared to Gideon, He uttered, "The Lord is with you, mighty warrior."

"But sir," Gideon replied, "if the Lord is with us, why has all this happened to us? Where are His wonders that our fathers told us about when they said, 'Did not the Lord bring us out of Egypt?' But now the Lord has abandoned us and put us into the hand of Midian."

The Lord then turned to him and said, "Go in the strength you have and save Israel out of Midian's hand. Am I not sending you?"

"But Lord," Gideon asked, "how can I save Israel? My clan is the weakest in Manasseh, and I am the least in my family."

The Lord answered, "I will be with you, and you will strike down the Midianites together."

¤ Is anything too difficult for the Lord? ¤ Ah, Lord God! Behold, You have made the heavens and the earth by Your great power and outstretched arm. There is nothing too hard for You. You show loving-kindness to thousands, and repay the iniquity of the fathers into the bosom of their children after them—the Great, the Mighty God, whose name is the Lord of Hosts. You are great in counsel and mighty in work, for your eyes are open to all the ways of the sons of men, to give everyone according to their ways and according to the fruit of his/her doings.

Judges 6:11-16, Genesis 18:14, Jeremiah 32:17-19

155

May 4th / November 4th

A champion named Goliath, who was from Gath, came out of the Philistine camp.

He was over nine feet tall... Goliath stood and shouted to the ranks of Israel, "Why do you come out and line up for battle? Am I not a Philistine, and are you not the servants of Saul? Choose a man and have him come down to me. If he is able to fight and kill me, we will become your subjects; but if I overcome him and kill him, you will become our subjects and serve us... This day I defy the ranks of Israel! Give me a man and let us fight each other."

On hearing the Philistine's words, Saul and all the Israelites were dismayed and terrified. ...But David said to Saul, "Let no one lose heart on account of this Philistine; your servant will go and fight him."

Saul replied, "You are not able to go out against this Philistine and fight him, for you are only a boy, and he has been a fighting man from his youth."

But David said to Saul... "The Lord who delivered me from the paw of the lion and the paw of the bear will deliver me from the hand of this Philistine."

...So David triumphed over the Philistine with just a sling and a stone; without a sword in his hand he struck down the Philistine and killed him. David then ran and stood over Goliath. He took hold of the Philistine's sword and drew it from the scabbard. After he killed him he cut off his head with the sword.

¤ The Lord loves the just and will not forsake His faithful ones. They will be protected forever, but the offspring of the wicked will be cut off; the righteous will inherit the land and dwell in it forever.

1st Samuel 17:4, 8-11, 32-34, 37, 50, 51, Psalm 37:28, 29

May 5th / November 5th

Now God gave Solomon wisdom and exceedingly great understanding, and breadth of heart like the sand that is on the seashore.

Thus Solomon's wisdom excelled the wisdom of all the sons of the east and all the wisdom of Egypt. For he was wiser than all men... and his fame was known in all the surrounding nations. He also spoke 3000 proverbs, and his songs were 1005. He spoke of trees; from the cedar that is in Lebanon even to the hyssop that grows on the wall. He spoke also of animals and birds and creeping things and fish. Men came from the peoples of all nations to hear the wisdom of Solomon; from all the kings of the earth who had heard of his wisdom.

¤ Now King Solomon loved many foreign women... From the nations which the Lord had said to the sons of Israel, "You shall not associate with them, nor shall they associate with you, for they will surely turn your heart away after their gods." Solomon held fast to these in love. He had seven hundred wives, princesses, and three hundred concubines, and his wives turned his heart away... His heart was not wholly devoted to the Lord his God.

¤ Therefore, be on your guard so that you are not carried away by the error of unprincipled men and fall from your own steadfastness. ¤ Let him who thinks he stands take heed that he does not fall. No temptation has overtaken you that is not common to man. And God is faithful; He will not let you be tempted beyond what you can bear. When you are tempted, He will also provide a way out so that you can stand up under it.

1st Kings 4:29-34, 1st Kings 11:1-4, 2nd Peter3:17, 1st Corinthians 10:12, 13

May 6th / November 6th

God said, "Let there be light," and there was light.

¤ No one, after lighting a lamp, puts it away in a cellar nor under a basket, but on the lamp stand, so that those who enter may see the light. The eye is the lamp of your body; when your eyes are good, your whole body is full of light; but when your eyes are bad, your body is also full of darkness. See to it, then, that the light within you is not darkness. Therefore, if your whole body is full of light, and no part of it is dark, it will be completely lighted, as when the light of a lamp shines upon you.

¤ The Lord is my light and my salvation; whom shall I fear? The Lord is the defense of my life; whom shall I dread? ¤ The Lord is God and He has given us light. ¤ The people who were sitting in darkness saw a great light, and those who were sitting in the shadow of death, upon them a light dawned.

¤ Jesus spoke to the people, saying, "I am the Light of the world; he who follows Me will not walk in the darkness, but will have the Light of life. ¤ We must work the works of Him who sent Me as long as it is day, for the night is coming when no one can work. While I am in the world, I am the Light of the world. ¤ For a little while longer the Light is among you. Walk while you have the Light, so that darkness will not overtake you; he who walks in the darkness does not know where he goes. While you have the Light, believe in the Light, so that you may become sons and daughters of Light."

Genesis 1:3, Luke 11:33-36, Psalm 27:1, Psalm 118:27,
Matthew 4:16, John 8:12, John 9:4, 5, John 12:35, 36

158

May 7th / November 7th

Though Jesus had performed many signs before them, they would still not believe in Him.

This was to fulfill the word of Isaiah the prophet which he spoke: "Lord, who has believed our report? And to whom has the arm of the Lord been revealed?" For this reason they could not believe, for Isaiah said again, "He has blinded their eyes and He hardened their hearts, so that they would not see with their eyes and perceive with their hearts, and be converted so that I might heal them."

These things Isaiah said because he saw His glory, and he spoke of Him. Yet at the same time many, even among the leaders, believed in Him. But because of the Pharisees they would not confess their faith, for fear they would be put out of the synagogue; for they loved the praise from men more than praise from God.

Then Jesus cried out, "When a man believes in Me, he does not believe in Me alone, but in the One who sent Me. When he looks at Me, he sees the One who sent Me. I have come into the world as a light, so that no one who believes in Me shall live in darkness. As for the person who hears My words but does not keep them, I do not judge him. For I did not come to judge the world, but to save it. There is a judge for the one who rejects Me and does not accept My words. And the very words which I speak will condemn him at the last day."

John 12:37-48

159

May 8ᵗʰ / November 8ᵗʰ

Whoever believes and is baptized will be saved.

¤ In the fifteenth year of the reign of Tiberius Caesar—when Pontius Pilate was governor of Judea, Herod being tetrarch of Galilee, his brother Philip tetrarch of Iturea and the region of Traconitis, and Lysanias tetrarch of Abilene—during the high priesthood of Annas and Caiaphas, the word of the Lord came to John, son of Zechariah, out in the desert. John then went into all the country around the Jordan, preaching a baptism of repentance for the forgiveness of sins. As it is written in the book of the words of Isaiah the prophet:

"The voice of one crying in the wilderness; 'Make ready the way of the Lord. Make His paths straight. Every ravine will be filled, and every mountain and hill will be brought low; the crooked paths will become straight, and the rough roads smooth; and all flesh will see the salvation of God.'"

And John began saying to the crowds who were going out to be baptized by him, "You brood of vipers, who warned you to flee from the wrath to come? Therefore bear fruits in keeping with repentance..." ¤ God is glorified by this, that you bear much fruit, and so prove to be followers of Jesus.

¤ Now you are Light in the Lord; walk as children of Light, for the fruit of the Light consists of all goodness and righteousness and truth, and trying to learn what is pleasing to the Lord. Do not participate in the unfruitful deeds of darkness, but rather expose them, for it is disgraceful even to speak of these things which are done by them in secret. But all things become visible when they are exposed by the Light... Therefore be careful how you walk, not as unwise people but as wise, making the most of your time, because the days are evil.

¤ For all of you who were baptized into Christ have clothed yourselves with Christ. ¤ Walk in the Light as He is in the Light.

160

Mark 16:16, Luke 3:1-8, John 15:8, Ephesians 5:8-13, 15, 16, Galatians 3:27, 1ˢᵗ John 1:7

May 9th / November 9th

The Spirit searches all things, even the deep things of God.

For who among men knows the thoughts of a man except the man's spirit within him? In the same way no one knows the thoughts of God except the Spirit of God. Now we have not received the spirit of the world, but the Spirit who is from God, that we may understand what God has freely given us.

This is what we speak, not in words taught us by human wisdom, but in words taught by the spirit; expressing spiritual truths in spiritual words. The man/woman without the Spirit does not accept the things that come from the Spirit of God, for they are foolishness to him/her, and they cannot understand them, because they are spiritually discerned. The spiritual man/woman makes appraisals about all things, but he/she are not subject to anyone's appraisal—not subject to the opinions of nonbelievers: For who has known the mind of the Lord that they can instruct Him? But we have the mind of Christ.

¤ The fruit of the Spirit is love, joy, peace, patience, kindness, goodness, faithfulness, gentleness, and self-control. Against such things there is no law. Now those who belong to Christ Jesus have crucified the flesh with its passions and desires. If we live by the Spirit, let us also walk by the Spirit. Let us not become boastful, challenging one another, envying one another. ¤ For just as the body without the spirit is dead, so also faith without works is dead.

1st Corinthians 2:10-16, Galatians 5:22-26, James 2:26

May 10th / November 10th

The tongue is a small part of the body, and yet it boasts of great things.

Consider what a great forest is set on fire by a small spark. The tongue also is a fire; a world of evil among the parts of the body. It corrupts the whole person, sets the whole course of his/her life on fire, as is itself set on fire by hell.

All kinds of animals, birds, reptiles and creatures of the sea are being tamed and have been tamed by man, but no man can tame the tongue. It is a restless evil, full of deadly poison. With our tongue we praise our Lord and Father, and with it we curse men, who have been made in the likeness of God. Out of the same mouth come both praise and cursing, and this should not be. Can both fresh water and salt water flow from the same spring? Can a fig tree bear olives, or a grapevine bear figs? Neither can a salt spring produce fresh water.

¤ Out of the overflow of the heart the mouth speaks. The good person brings good things out of the good stored up in them, and the evil person brings evil things out of the evil stored up in them. But I tell you that people will have to give an account on the day of judgment for every careless word they have spoken. For by your words you will be acquitted, and by your words your will be condemned.

¤ Your own mouth condemns you, and your own lips testify against you. ¤ Wise men store up knowledge, but with the mouth of the foolish, ruin is at hand. ¤ Death and life are in the power of the tongue, and those who love it will eat of its fruit.

¤ We all stumble in many ways. If anyone is never at fault in what they say, they become perfect, able to keep the whole body in check.

James 3:5-12, Matthew 12:34-37, Job 15:6, Proverbs 10:14, Proverbs 18:21, James 3:2

May 11ᵗʰ / November 11ᵗʰ

Those who feared the Lord spoke often of Him to one another...

And the Lord gave attention and heard it, and a book of remembrance was written before Him for those who fear the Lord and esteem His name. "They will be mine," says the Lord of hosts, "and on the day that I prepare My own possession, I will spare them as a man spares his own children who serve him." So you will again see the distinction between the righteous and the wicked; between those who serve God, and those who do not.

¤ Jesus said, "Where two or three come together in My name, there I am with them." ¤ Let the words of Christ dwell in you richly, and admonish one another with all wisdom as you sing psalms, hymns and spiritual songs with gratitude in your hearts to God. And whatever you do, whether in word or deed, do it all in the name of the Lord Jesus, giving thanks to God the Father through Him.

¤ Encourage one another daily, as long as it is called today, so that none of you may become hardened by the deceitfulness of sin. ¤ The commandments I have given you are to be upon your hearts. Impress them on your children. Talk about them when you sit at home and when you walk along the road, when you lie down at night and when you rise in the morning. Tie them as symbols on your hands and bind them on your foreheads. Write them on the door frames of your houses and on your gates.

¤ Do not be wise in your own eyes; fear the Lord and turn away from evil.

Malachi 3:16-18, Matthew 18:20, Colossians 3:16, 17, Hebrews 3:13, Deuteronomy 6:6-9, Proverbs 3:7

May 12th
November 12th

And the Lord says, "I am your portion and your inheritance."

¤ Whom have I in heaven but You? And besides You, I desire nothing on earth. My flesh and my heart may fail, but God is the strength of my heart and my portion forever. For behold, those who are far from You will perish; You have destroyed all those who are unfaithful to You. But as for me, the nearness of God is my good; I have made the Lord God my refuge, that I may tell of Your works.

¤ The Lord is the portion of my inheritance and my cup; You have made my lot secure. The boundary lines have fallen for me in pleasant places; surely I have a delightful inheritance. ¤ I say to myself, "The Lord is my portion; therefore I will wait for Him." The Lord is good to those whose hope is in Him; to the one who seeks Him. It is good to wait quietly for the salvation of the Lord.

¤ Your statutes are my heritage forever; they are the joy of my heart. My heart is set on keeping Your decrees to the very end. I hate double-minded men, but I love Your law. You are my refuge and my shield; I have put my hope in Your word.

¤ When I remember You on my bed, I meditate on You during the watches of the night. For You have been my help, and in the shadow of Your wings I sing for joy. My soul clings to You; Your right hand upholds me. ¤ In God I have put my trust, I shall not be afraid.

Numbers 18:20, Psalm 73:25-28, Psalm 16:5, 6, Lamentations 3:24-26, Psalm 119:113, 114, Psalm 63:6-8 & 56:11

May 13th
November 13th

Who can say, "I have kept my heart pure; I am clean and without sin"?

¤ The Lord looks down from heaven on the sons of men to see if there are any who understand, any who seek God. All have turned aside, they have together become corrupt; there is no one who does good, not even one. ¤ The sinful mind is hostile toward God. It does not submit to God's law, nor can it do so. Those controlled by their sinful nature cannot please God.

¤ I know that nothing good lives in me, that is, in my sinful nature. I have the desire to do what is good, but I cannot carry it out. For what I do is not the good I want to do; no, the evil I do not want to do—this I keep on doing. ¤ All of us have become like one who is unclean, and all of our righteous acts are like filthy rags. All of us wither like a leaf, and like the wind our iniquities sweep us away.

¤ The Scriptures declare that the whole world is a prisoner of sin. ¤ But if anyone is in Christ, he/she is a new creature; the old things have passed away, and new things have come! And all these wondrous things are from God, who reconciled us to Himself through Christ by the ministry of reconciliation, namely, that God was in Christ reconciling the world to Himself, not counting their sins against them. ¤ If the Son has set you free, then you shall be free indeed!

Proverbs 20:9, Psalm 14:2, 3, Romans 8:7, 8, Romans 7:18, 19, Isaiah 64:6, Galatians 3:22, 2nd Corinthians 5:17-19, John 8:36

May 14th / November 14th

Differing weights and differing measures—the Lord detests them both.

◻ The Lord abhors dishonest scales, but accurate weights are His delight. ◻ Do your rulers indeed speak justly? Do you judge uprightly among men? No, in your heart you devise injustice, and your hands mete out violence on the earth.

◻ How long will you defend the unjust and show partiality to the wicked? Defend instead the cause of the weak and fatherless; maintain the rights of the poor and oppressed. Rescue the weak and needy; deliver them from the hand of the wicked.

◻ Do not judge, or you too will be judged. For in the same way you judge others, you will be judged, and with the measure you use, it will be measured unto you. Why do you look at the speck of sawdust in your brother's or sister's eye, and yet pay no attention to the plank that's in your own eye?

How can you say to your brother/sister, "Let me take the speck our of your eye," when all the time there is a plank in your own eye? You hypocrite, first take the plank out of your own eye, and then you will see clearly to remove the speck from your brother's/sister's eye. ◻ Stop judging by mere appearances, and make a righteous judgment.

◻ For we will all stand before God's judgment seat. It is written: "As surely as I live," says the Lord, "every knee will bow before Me; every tongue will confess to God."

So then, each of us will give an account of himself/herself to God. Therefore let us stop passing judgment on one another.

Proverbs 20:10, Proverbs 11:1, Psalm 58:1, 2, Psalm 82:2-4, Matthew 7:1-5, John 7:24, Romans 14:10-13

May 15th / November 15th

"Have faith in God," Jesus answered.

"I tell your the truth, if anyone says to this mountain, 'Go, throw yourself into the sea,' and does not doubt in his/her heart but believes that what is said will happen, then it will be done for them. Whatever you ask in prayer, believe that you have received it, and it will be yours. And when you stand praying, if you hold anything against anyone, forgive them, so that your Father in heaven may forgive you your sins."

¤ Jesus said, "A man was going down from Jerusalem to Jericho, when he fell into the hands of robbers. They stripped him of his clothes, beat him and went away, leaving him half dead. A priest happened to be going down the same road, and when he saw the man, he passed by on the other side. So too, a Levite, when he came to the place and saw him, passed by on the other side.

"But a Samaritan, as he traveled, came where the man was; and when he saw him, he took pity on him. He went to him and bandaged his wounds, pouring on oil and wine. Then he put the man on his own donkey, took him to an inn and took care of him. The next day he took out two silver coins and gave them to the innkeeper. 'Look after him,' he said, 'and when I return, I will reimburse you for any extra expense that you may have.'

"Which of these three do you think was a neighbor to the man who fell into the hands of robbers?"

An expert in the law replied, "The one who had mercy on him."

Jesus then told him, "Go and do likewise."

Mark 11:22-26, Luke 10:30-37

May 16th / November 16th

You are not to go back that way again.

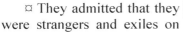 They admitted that they were strangers and exiles on the earth. People who say such things show that they are looking for a country of their own. If they had been thinking of the country they had left, they would have had opportunity to return. Instead they were longing for a better country—a heavenly one. Therefore God is not ashamed to be called their God, for He has prepared a place for them...

By faith Moses left Egypt, not fearing the king's anger; he persevered because he saw Him who is invisible. ¤ He who is coming will come and will not delay. "My righteous one will live by faith," says the Lord. "And if he shrinks back, My soul has no pleasure in him." Do not be of those who shrink back and are destroyed, but be of those who believe and are saved.

¤ Do not be yoked together with unbelievers. For what do righteousness and wickedness have in common? Or what fellowship can light have with darkness?... What does a believer have in common with an unbeliever? ... As God has said, ... "Come out from among them and be separate. Touch no unclean thing, and I will receive you. I will be a Father to you, and you will be My sons and daughters."

Since we have these promises, let us purify ourselves from everything that contaminates body and spirit, perfecting holiness out of reverence for God. ¤ He who began a good work in you will surely perfect it until the day of Christ Jesus.

Deuteronomy 17:16, Hebrews 11:13-16, 27, Hebrews 10:37-39,
2nd Corinthians 6:14-18 & 7:1, Philippians 1:6

May 17th / November 17th

By faith we understand that the universe was formed at God's command.

By faith Abel offered God a better sacrifice than Cain did, and was commended as a righteous man. By faith Enoch was taken from this life, so that he did not experience death; he could not be found, because God had taken him away. By faith Noah, when warned about things not yet seen, built an ark to save his family. By his faith he condemned the world and became an heir of the righteousness that comes by faith.

By faith Abraham, when called to go to a place that he would later receive as his inheritance, obeyed and went, even though he did not know where he was going. By faith he made his home in the promised land like a stranger in a foreign country; he lived in tents, as did Isaac and Jacob, who were heirs with him in the same promise. For he was looking forward to the city with foundations, whose architect and builder is God.

These people were still living by faith when they died. They did not receive the things promised; they only saw them and welcomed them from a distance. And they admitted that they were strangers and exiles on the earth.

¤ For it is by grace that you have been saved, through faith —and this is not from yourselves, it is the gift of God—not by works, so that no one can boast. For we are God's workmanship, created in Christ Jesus to do good deeds, which God prepared in advance for us to do... Consequentially, you are no longer foreigners and exiles, but fellow citizens with God's people and members of His household; built on the foundation of the apostles and prophets, with Christ Jesus Himself as the chief cornerstone.

Hebrews 11:3-10, 13, Ephesians 2:8-10, 19, 20

May 18th / November 18th

Be completely humble and gentle;

Be patient, bearing with one another in love. Make every effort to keep the unity of the Spirit through the bond of peace. There is one body and one Spirit—just as you were called to one hope when you were called—one Lord, one faith, one baptism; one God and Father of all, who is over all and through all and in all. But to each one of us grace has been given as Christ apportioned it. This is why the Scriptures say:

"When He ascended on high, He led captives in His train and gave gifts to men."

¤ Since you died with Christ to the basic principles of this world, why then as though you still belonged to it, do you submit to its rules: "Do not handle! Do not taste! Do not touch!" These are all destined to perish with use, because they are based on human commands and teachings. These are matters which have, to be sure, the appearance of wisdom in self-made religion and self-abasement and severe treatment of the body, *but are* of *no* value against fleshly indulgence...

Since, then, you have been raised with Christ, set your hearts on things above, where Christ is seated at the right hand of God. Set your minds on things above, not on earthly things. For you died, and your life is now hidden with Christ in God. When Christ, who is you life, appears, then you will also appear with Him in glory.

Ephesians 4:2-8, Colossians 2:20-23, & 3:1-4

171

May 19ᵗʰ / November 19ᵗʰ

Forsake your folly and live, and proceed in the way of understanding.

¤ It is God's will that you should be sanctified: that you should avoid sexual immorality; that each of you should learn to control his/her own body in a way that is holy and honorable, not in passionate lust like the heathen, who do not know God; and that in this matter no one should wrong another or take advantage of them. The Lord will punish people for all such sins, as we have already told you and warned you.

For God did not call us to be impure, but to live a holy life. Therefore he/she who rejects this instruction does not reject man but God, who gives you His Holy Spirit. ¤ God's solid foundation stands firm, sealed with this inscription: "The Lord knows those who are His", and, "Everyone who confesses the name of the Lord must turn away from wickedness." ... Flee the evil desires of youth and pursue righteousness, faith, love and peace, along with those who call on the Lord out of a pure heart.

Don't have anything to do with foolish and stupid, arguments, because you know that they produce quarrels. And the Lord's servant must not quarrel; instead he/she must be kind to everyone, able to teach, not resentful. Those who oppose you must be gently instructed, in the hope that God will grant them repentance leading them to a knowledge of the truth, and that they will come to their senses and escape from the trap of the devil, who has taken them captive to do his will.

¤ Be self-controlled and alert. Your enemy the devil prowls around like a roaring lion looking for someone to devour. Resist him, standing firm in the faith.

Proverbs 9:6, 1ˢᵗ Thessalonians 4:3-8, 2ⁿᵈ Timothy 2:19, 22-26,
1ˢᵗ Peter 5:8, 9

May 20th / November 20th

The Word of Life appeared; we have seen it and testify to it...

This is the message we have heard from Him and declare to you. God is light; in Him there is no darkness at all. If we claim to have fellowship with Him yet walk in the darkness, we lie and do not live by the truth. But if we walk in the light, as He is in the light, we have fellowship with one another, and the blood of Jesus, His son, purifies us from all sin.

If we claim to be without sin, we deceive ourselves and the truth is not in us. If we confess our sins, He is faithful and just and will forgive us our sins and purify us from all unrighteousness. If we claim we have not sinned, we make Him out to be a liar and His word has no place in our lives...

We know that we have come to know Him if we obey His commands. The person who says, "I know Him," but does not do what He commands is a liar, and the truth is not in them. But if anyone obeys His word, God's love is truly made complete in him/her. This is how we know that we are in Him: Whoever claims to live in Him must walk as Jesus did.

¤ Bless the Lord, O my soul, and forget not His benefits; Who pardons all of your iniquities, Who heals all of your diseases; Who redeems your life from the pit, Who crowns you with loving-kindness and compassion; Who satisfies your years with good things, so that your youth is renewed like the eagle.

1st John 1:2, 5-10 & 2:3-6, Psalm 103:2-5

May 21ˢᵗ / November 21ˢᵗ

Blessed are those who do not walk in the counsel of the wicked, nor stand in the path of sinners, nor sit in the seat of mockers.

But their delight is in the law of the Lord, and on His law they meditate day and night. They are like trees planted by streams of water, which yield their fruit in season. Their leaves do not wither, and in whatever they do they will prosper.

¤ Let all who take refuge in You be glad; let them ever sing for joy. Spread Your protection over them, that those who love Your name may rejoice in You. For surely, O Lord, You bless the righteous; You surround them with Your favor as with a shield.

¤ You hear, O Lord, the desire of the afflicted; You encourage them, and You listen to their cry, defending the fatherless and the oppressed, in order that man, who is of the earth, may terrify them no more.

¤ The heavens declare the glory of God; the skies proclaim the work of His hands. Day after day they pour forth speech; night after night they display knowledge. There is no speech or language where their voice is not heard. Their voice goes out into all the earth, their words to the end of the world... The law of the Lord is perfect, reviving the soul. The statutes of the Lord are trustworthy, making wise the simple.

The precepts of the Lord are right, giving joy to the heart. The commands of the Lord are radiant, giving light to the eyes... By them Your servant is warned, and in keeping them there is great reward.

Psalm 1:1-3, Psalm 5:11, 12, Psalm 10:17, 18, Psalm 19:1-4, 7, 8, 11

May 22nd / November 22nd

And the Lord said to Job:

"Will the one who contends with the Almighty correct Him? Let Him who accuses God answer Him!"

Then Job answered the Lord: "I am unworthy—how can I reply to You? I put my hand over my mouth. I spoke once, but I have no answer—twice, but I will say no more."

Then the Lord spoke to Job out of the storm: "Brace yourself like a man; I will question you, and you shall answer Me. Would you discredit My justice? Would you condemn Me to justify yourself? Do you have an arm like God's, and can you voice thunder like His? Then adorn yourself with glory and splendor, and clothe yourself in honor and majesty.

"Unleash the fury of your wrath, look at every proud man and bring him low, look at every proud man and humble him, and crush the wicked where they stand. Bury them all in the dust together; shroud their faces in the grave. Then I Myself will admit to you that your own right hand can save you... Who has a claim against Me that I must pay? Everything under heaven belongs to Me."

...Then the Lord blessed the latter part of Job's life more than the first... After this Job lived a hundred and forty years; he saw his children and their children to the fourth generation.

¤ Even when I am old and gray, do not forsake me, O God, until I declare Your power to the next generation, your Might to all who are to come.

Job 40:1-14 & 41:11 & 42:12, 16, Psalm 71:18

May 23rd / November 23rd

Blessed is a person who fears the Lord...

One who finds great delight in His commands. His/her children will be mighty in the land; the generation of the upright will be blessed. Wealth and riches are in their house, and their righteousness endures forever. Even in darkness light dawns for the upright, for the gracious and compassionate and righteous person. Good will come to those who are generous and lend freely, who conduct their affairs with justice.

Surely they will never be shaken; a righteous person will be remembered forever. They will have no fear of bad news; their heart is steadfast, trusting in the Lord. Their heart is secure; they will have no fear, and in the end they will look in triumph on their foes. They have also scattered abroad their gifts to the poor, their righteousness endures forever...

The wicked man/woman will see and be vexed, they will gnash their teeth and waste away; the longings of the wicked will come to nothing.

¤ The Lord spoke to me with a strong hand upon me, warning me not to follow the way of the people. He said:

"Do not call conspiracy everything that these people call conspiracy. Do not fear what they fear, and do not dread it. The Lord Almighty is the one you are to regard as holy, and He is the one you are to fear, He is the one you are to dread, and He will be a sanctuary." ¤ Trust in the Lord with all your heart, and lean not on your own understanding.

Psalm 112, Isaiah 8:11-14, Proverbs 3:5

May 24th / November 24th

*The end of a matter is
better than its beginning.*

And patience is better
than pride. Do not be quickly
provoked in your spirit, for anger resides in the lap of fools. Do
not say, "Why were the old days better than these?" For it is not
wise to ask such questions.

Wisdom, like an inheritance, is a good thing and benefits
those who see the sun. Wisdom is a shelter as money is a shelter,
but the advantage of knowledge is this: that wisdom preserves
the life of its possessor.

Who can straighten what he has made crooked? When times
are good, be happy; but when times are bad, consider: God has
made the one as well as the other. Therefore a man/woman
cannot discover anything about their future.

¤ A voice said, "Cry out." And I said, "What shall I cry?"
"That all men are like grass, and all of their glory is like the
flowers of the field. The grass withers and the flowers fall,
because the breath of the Lord blows on them. Surely the people
are grass. The grass withers and the flowers fall, but the word of
our God stands forever."

¤ Therefore this is what the Lord Almighty says: "See, I will
refine and test them, for what else can I do because of the sins of
My people? Their tongues are deadly arrows, speaking with
deceit. With their mouth each speaks cordially with their
neighbor, but in their hearts they set a trap for them. Should I
not punish them for this? Should I not avenge Myself on such a
nation as this?" ...Who is a wise man/woman, that they might
understand this?

Ecclesiastes 7:8-14, Isaiah 40:6-8, Jeremiah 9:7-9, 12

May 25th / November 25th

In the last days scoffers will come...

They will be scoffing and following after their own evil desires. They will say, "Where is this 'coming' that He promised? For ever since our fathers died, everything goes on as it has since the beginning of creation."

But they deliberately forget that long ago by God's word the heavens existed and the earth was formed out of water and by water. By these waters also the world of that time was deluged and destroyed. By the same word the present heavens and earth are reserved for fire, being kept for the day of judgment and destruction of ungodly men.

But do not forget one thing, dear friends: With the Lord a day is like a thousand years and a thousand years are like a day. The Lord is not slow in keeping His promise, as some understand slowness. Yet He is patient with you, not wanting anyone to perish, but that all would come to repentance.

And the day of the Lord will come like a thief. The heavens will disappear with a roar; the elements will be destroyed by fire, and the earth and everything in it will be laid bare. Since everything will be destroyed in this way, what kind of people ought you to be? You ought to live holy and godly lives as you look forward to the day of God and speed its coming.

That day of course will bring about the destruction of the heavens by fire, and the elements will melt in the heat. But in keeping with His promise, we are looking forward to a new heaven and a new earth, the home of righteousness.

2nd Peter 3:3-13

May 26th / November 26th

Bear in mind that our Lord's patience means salvation.

Paul wrote of this with the wisdom that God gave him. He writes the same way in all of his letters, speaking in them of these matters. His letters do contain some things that are hard to understand, which the ignorant and unstable people distort, as they do the other Scriptures, to their own destruction.

Therefore, dear friends, since you already know this, be on your guard so that you may not be carried away by the error of lawless people, and fall from your secure position. But grow in grace and knowledge of our Lord and Savior Jesus Christ. To Him be glory both now and forever.

¤ From the beginning God chose you to be saved through the sanctifying work of the Spirit and through your belief in the truth. He called you to this through our gospel, that you might share in the glory of our Lord Jesus Christ. So then, brothers and sisters, stand firm and hold to the teachings we passed on to you, whether by word of mouth or by letter.

May our Lord Jesus Christ Himself and God our Father, who loved us and by His grace gave us eternal encouragement and good hope, encourage your hearts and strengthen you in every good deed and word.

¤ Do your best to present yourselves to God as one approved; a person who does not need to be ashamed, and one who correctly handles the word of truth.

2nd Peter 3:15-18, 2nd Thessalonians 2:13-17, 2nd Timothy 2:15

179

May 27th / November 27th

How great is the love the Father has lavished on us, that we should be called children of God!

And that is what we are! The reason that the world does not know us is that it did not know Him. Dear friends, now we are children of God, and what we will be has not yet been made known. But we know that when He appears, we shall be like Him, for we shall see Him as He is. Everyone who has this hope within themselves purifies himself/herself, just as He is pure.

Everyone who sins breaks the law; in fact, sin is lawlessness. But you know that He appeared so that He might take away our sins. And in Him is no sin. No one who lives in Him keeps on sinning. No one who continues to sin has either seen Him or known Him. Do not let anyone lead you astray. He who endeavors to do what is right is righteous, just as He is righteous. But he who continues to do what is sinful is of the devil, because the devil has been sinning from the beginning.

The reason the Son of God appeared was to destroy the devil's work. No one who is born of God will continue to sin, because God's seed remains in him/her; they cannot go on sinning, because he/she has been born of God. This is how we know who the children of God are and who the children of the devil are: Anyone who continues to do what is not right is not a child of God; nor is anyone who does not love his brother/sister.

¤ Keep yourselves in God's love as you wait for the mercy of our Lord Jesus Christ to bring you to eternal life.

1st John 3:1-10, Jude 21

180

May 28th / November 28th

John saw Jesus coming toward him, and said, "Behold the Lamb of God, who takes away the sin of the world!"

¤ After this I looked and there before me was a great multitude that no one could count, from every nation, tribe, people and language, standing before the throne and in front of the Lamb. They were wearing white robes and were holding palm branches in their hands. And they cried out in a loud voice: "Salvation belongs to our God, who sits on the throne, and to the Lamb."

¤ He went to Nazareth, where He had been brought up, and on the Sabbath day He went into the synagogue, as was His custom. And He stood up to read. The scroll of the prophet Isaiah was handed to Him. Unrolling it, He found the place where it is written:

"The Spirit of the Lord is upon Me, because He has anointed Me to preach the good news to the poor. He has sent Me to proclaim freedom for the prisoners and recovery of sight for the blind, to release the oppressed, and to proclaim the year of the Lord's favor."

Then He rolled up the scroll, gave it back to the attendant and sat down. The eyes of everyone in the synagogue were fastened on Him, and He began by saying to them, "Today, this Scripture is fulfilled in your hearing."

¤ "For I have come down from heaven, not to do My will, but to do the will of Him who sent Me."

John 1:29, Revelation 7:9, 10, Luke 4:16-21, John 6:38

181

May 29ᵗʰ / November 29ᵗʰ

As the crowds increased, Jesus said, "This is a wicked generation.

"It asks for a miraculous sign, but none will be given it except the sign of Jonah. For as Jonah was a sign to the Ninevites, so also will the Son of Man be to this generation. The Queen of the South will rise at the judgment with the men/women of this generation and condemn them; for she came from the ends of the earth to listen to Solomon's wisdom, and now one greater than Solomon is here. The men/women of Nineveh will stand up at the judgment with this same generation and condemn it; for they repented at the preaching of Jonah, and now One greater than Jonah is here."

¤ Again He said, "What shall we say the kingdom of God is like, or what parable shall we use to describe it? It is like a mustard seed, which is the smallest seed that you can plant in the ground. Yet when planted, it grows and becomes the largest of all garden plants, with such big branches that the birds of the air can perch in its shade."

¤ When He came near the place where the road goes down to the Mount of Olives, the whole crowd of disciples began joyfully to praise God in loud voices for all the miracles they had seen: "Blessed is the king who comes in the name of the Lord! Peace in heaven and glory in the highest!"

Some of the Pharisees in the crowd said to Jesus, "Teacher, rebuke your disciples!"

"I tell you," He responded, "if they keep silent, the stones on the ground will cry out."

Luke 11:29-32, Mark 4:30-32, Luke 19:37-40

May 30th / November 30th

"Tell us by what authority You are doing these things?

"Who gave You this authority?" the chief priests and the elders questioned.

Jesus then replied, "I will ask you a question. Tell me, of John's baptism—was it from heaven or from men?"

They discussed it among themselves, and then said, "If we say, 'From heaven,' He will ask, 'Why didn't you believe him?' But if we say, 'From men,' all the people will stone us, because they are persuaded that John was a prophet." And so they answered Him, "We do not know where it was from."

Jesus said, "Neither then will I tell you by what authority I am doing these things."

...While all the people were listening, Jesus said to His disciples, "Beware of the teachers of the law. They like to walk around in flowing robes, and love to be greeted in the marketplaces, and have the most important seats in the synagogues, and the places of honor at banquets. They devour widows' houses, and for a show make lengthy prayers. Such men will receive greater condemnation."

¤ Once again the kingdom of heaven is like a net that was let down into the lake and caught all kinds of fish. When the net was full, the fishermen pulled it up onto the shore. Then they sat down and collected the good fish in baskets, but threw the bad ones away. This is how it will be at the end of the age. The angels will come and separate the wicked from the righteous and throw them into the fiery furnace, where there will be weeping and gnashing of teeth.

Luke20:2-8, & 20:45-47, Matthew 13:47-50

May 31ˢᵗ

When you have done everything you were told to do, you should say, 'We are unworthy servants; we have only done our duty.'

¤ So then, what can we boast about doing to earn our salvation? Nothing at all. Why? Because our acquittal is not based on our good deeds—it is based on what Christ has done and our faith in Him. ¤ What makes you different than anyone else? What do you have that God hasn't given to you? And if all that you have is from God, why do you act as though you are so great, and as though you have accomplished something good on your own?

¤ For it is by grace that you have been saved, through faith —and this is not from yourselves; it is the gift of God. Salvation is not a reward for any good that we might do, so none of us can take any credit for it. It is God Himself who made us what we are and given us new lives from Christ Jesus—and in long ago ages He planned that we should spend these lives of ours in helping others.

¤ Whatever we are now it is all because God poured out such kindness, mercy and grace upon us. ¤ For everything comes from God alone. Everything lives by His power, and everything is for His glory. ¤ Again, everything comes from God, and we only can have and in turn give to others what has come from His hand.

¤ "Come now, let us reason together," says the Lord. "Though your sins are like scarlet, they shall be as white as snow; though they are red as crimson, they shall be like wool. If you are willing and obedient, you will eat the best from the land." ¤ "I will give you a new heart and put a new spirit within you. I will remove from you your heart of stone... and I will put My Spirit within you, and move you to follow My decrees."

Luke 17:10, Romans 3: 27, 28, 1ˢᵗ Corinthians 4:7, Ephesians 2:8-10, 1ˢᵗ Corinthians 15:10, Romans 11:36, 1ˢᵗ Chronicles 29:14, Isaiah 1:18-20, Ezekiel 36:26, 27

June 1st / December 1st

The Lord gives wisdom, and from His mouth come knowledge and understanding.

He holds victory in store for the upright, He is a shield to those whose walk is blameless, for He guards the course of the just and protects the way of His faithful ones. You will understand what is right and just and fair—every good path. For wisdom will enter your heart, and knowledge will be pleasant to your soul. Discretion will protect you, and understanding will guard you.

Wisdom will save you from the ways of wicked men, from men whose words are perverse, who leave the straight paths to walk in dark ways, who delight in doing wrong and rejoice in the perverseness of evil, whose paths are crooked and who are devious in their ways.

¤ Wisdom has built her house; she has hewn out its seven pillars. She has prepared her meat and mixed her wine; she has also set her table. She has sent out her maids and she calls from the highest point of the city.

"Let all who are simple come in here!" she says to those who lack judgment. "Come, eat my food and drink the wine I have mixed. Leave your simple ways and you will live; walk in the way of understanding."

¤ The idols of the nations are silver and gold, made by the hands of men. They have mouths, but cannot speak, eyes, but they cannot see; they have ears, but cannot hear, nor is there breath in their mouths. Those who make them will be like them, and so will all who trust in them.

Proverbs 2:6-15, Proverbs 9:1-6, Psalm 135:15-18

186

June 2nd / December 2nd

There will be no more gloom for those who are in distress.

In the past He humbled the land of Zebulun and the land of Naphtali, but in the future He will honor Galilee of the Gentiles, by way of the sea, along the Jordan—the people walking in darkness will see a great light; on those living in the land of the shadow of death a light will dawn.

And He will be called Wonderful, Counselor, the Mighty God, the Everlasting Father, the Prince of Peace. Of the increase of His government and peace there shall be no end. He will reign on David's throne and over His kingdom, establishing and upholding it with justice and righteousness from that time and on forever. The zeal of the Lord Almighty will accomplish this.

¤ "This is the covenant that I will make with My people after that time," declares the Lord. "I will put My law in their minds and write it upon their hearts. I will be their God, and they will be My people. No longer will a man teach his neighbor or a man his brother, saying, 'Know the Lord,' because they will all know Me, from the least of them to the greatest. For I will forgive their wickedness and will remember their sins no more."

¤ "I will accept them as fragrant incense when I bring them out from the nations and gather them from the countries where they have been scattered, and I will show Myself holy among them in the sight of the nations... They they will know that I am the Lord, when I deal with them for My name's sake, and not according to their evil ways and corrupt practices."

Isaiah 9:1, 2, 6, 7, Jeremiah 31:33, 34, Ezekiel 20:41, 44

187

June 3rd / December 3rd

His mercy extends to those who fear Him, from generation to generation.

He has performed mighty deeds with His arm; He has scattered those who are proud in their inmost thoughts. He has brought down rulers from their thrones, but has lifted up the humble. He has filled the hungry with good things, but has sent the rich away empty. He has helped His servants, remembering to be merciful to Abraham and his descendants forever, even as He has said to our fathers...

Praise be to the Lord, the God of Israel, because He has come and has redeemed His people. He has raised up a horn of salvation for us in the house of His servant David (as He said through His holy prophets of long ago), salvation from our enemies and from the hand of all who hate us—to show mercy to our fathers and to remember His holy covenant, the oath He swore to Abraham:

To rescue us from the hand of our enemies, and to enable us to serve Him without fear in holiness and righteousness before Him all of our days.

¤ And there were shepherds living out in the fields nearby, keeping watch over their flocks by night. An angel of the Lord appeared to them, and they were terrified. But the angel said to them, "Do not be afraid, for I bring you good tidings of great joy that will be for all the people. Today in the town of David a Savior has been born to you; You will find a baby wrapped in cloths and lying in a manger."

Luke 1:50-55, 68-75, Luke 2:8-12

June 4th / December 4th

*Suddenly a great company
of the heavenly host
appeared with the angel.*

And they praised God, saying, "Glory to God in the highest, and to earth peace on all upon whom His favor rests."

When the angels had departed from the shepherds and gone into heaven, the men said to one another, "Let us go to Bethlehem and see this thing that has happened, which the Lord has told us about."

And so they hurried off and found Mary and Joseph, and the baby, who was lying in the manger. When they had seen Him, they spread the word concerning what had been told them about this Child, and all who heard it were amazed at what the shepherds said to them.

But Mary treasured all these things and pondered them in her heart. The shepherds returned to the fields, glorifying and praising God for all the things they had heard and seen, which were just as they had been told.

¤ After Jesus was born in Bethlehem of Judea, in the days of Herod the king, wise men from the east arrived in Jerusalem, and they asked, "Where is the One who has been born King of the Jews? For we saw His star in the east, and have come to worship Him."

¤ I see Him, but not now; I behold Him, but not near. A star shall come forth from Jacob; a scepter shall rise out of Israel.

¤ You are to give Him the name Jesus. He will be great and will be called the Son of the Most High.

Luke 2:13-20, Matthew 2:1, 2, Numbers 24:17, Luke 1:31, 32

189

June 5th / December 5th

The scepter shall not depart from Judah, nor the rulers staff from between his feet, until Shiloh comes, and to Him shall be the obedience of all the people.

¤ When King Herod heard this he was disturbed, and all Jerusalem with him. When he had called together all the people's chief priests and teachers of the law, he asked them where the Christ was to be born.

"In Bethlehem of Judea," they replied, "for this is what the prophet has written: "But you, O Bethlehem, in the land of Judah, are by no means least among the rulers of Judah; for out of you will come forth a Ruler who will be the Shepherd of My people Israel."

Then Herod secretly called the wise men and determined from them the exact time that the star had appeared. And he sent them to Bethlehem and said, "Go and search carefully for the Child; and when you have found Him, report to me, so that I too may come and worship Him."

After hearing the king, they went their way; and the star, which they had seen in the east, went on before them until it came and stood over the place where the Child was. When they saw the star, they rejoiced exceedingly with great joy! After coming to the house they saw the Child with Mary His mother; and they fell to the ground and worshiped Him.

Then, opening their treasures, the wise men presented to Him gifts of gold, frankincense, and myrrh. And having been warned by God in a dream not to return to Herod, they left for their own country by another way.

Genesis 49:10, Matthew 2:3-12

190

June 6th / December 6th

*An angel of the Lord appeared
to Joseph in a dream.*

"Get up! Take the Child and His mother and flee to Egypt, and remain there until I tell you; for Herod is going to search for the Child to destroy Him."

So Joseph got up and took the Child and His mother while it was still night, and left for Egypt. He remained there until the death of Herod. This was to fulfill what had been spoken by the Lord through the prophet: "Out of Egypt I have called my Son."

When Herod saw that he had been tricked by the wise men, he became very enraged, and sent and slew all the male children who were in Bethlehem and all its vicinity, from two years old and under, according to the time which he had determined from the wise men. Then what had been spoken through Jeremiah the prophet was fulfilled:

"A voice was heard in Ramah, weeping and great mourning, Rachael weeping for her children; and she refused to be comforted, because they were no more."

But when Herod died, behold, and angel of the Lord appeared in a dream to Joseph in Egypt, and said, "Get up, take the Child and His mother, and go into the land of Israel; for those who sought the Child's life are dead."

So Joseph got up, took the Child and His mother, and came into the land of Israel. But when he heard that Archelaus was reigning over Judea in place of his father Herod, he was afraid to go there. Then after being warned by God in a dream, he left for the regions of Galilee, and came and lived in a city called Nazareth. This was to fulfill what was spoken through the prophets: "He shall be called a Nazarene."

Matthew 2:13-23

June 7th / December 7th

The Child continued to grow and become strong, increasing in wisdom; and the grace of God was upon Him.

Now His parents went to Jerusalem every year at the Feast of the Passover. And when Jesus became twelve years of age, they went up there according to the custom of the Feast; and as they were returning, after spending the full number of days, the boy Jesus stayed behind in Jerusalem. But His parents were unaware of this, and supposed Him to be in the caravan. After a day's journey they began searching for Him among their relatives and acquaintances. When they did not find Him, they returned to Jerusalem to look for Him.

After three days they found Him in the temple, sitting in the midst of the teachers; both listening to them and asking them questions. And all who heard Him were amazed at His understanding and His answers. When His parents saw Him, they were astonished; and His mother said to Him, "Son, why have You treated us this way? Your father and I have been anxiously looking for You."

And Jesus said to them, "Why is it that you were looking for Me? Did you not know that I had to be in My Father's house?"

But they did not understand the statement which He had made to them. And so He went down with them and came to Nazareth, and He continued in subjection to them; and His mother treasured all these things within her heart. And Jesus kept increasing in wisdom and stature, and in favor with God and men. ¤ When He began His ministry, Jesus Himself was about thirty years of age.

Luke 2:40-52, Luke 3:23

192

June 8th / December 8th

Then Jesus arrived from Galilee at the Jordan coming to John, to be baptized by him.

But John tried to prevent Him, saying, "I have need to be baptized by You, and do You come to me?"

But Jesus answering said to him, "Permit it at this time; for in this way it is fitting for us to fulfill all righteousness."

Then John permitted Him. After being baptized, Jesus came up immediately from the water, and behold, the heavens were opened, and John saw the Spirit of God descending as a dove and lighting upon Him, and a voice out of the heavens said, "This is My beloved Son, in whom I am well pleased."

¤ Jesus sometime later said to His followers, "Go into all the world and preach the gospel to all creation. He/she who has believed and has been baptized shall be saved; but he/she who has disbelieved shall be condemned."

¤ And Peter said to the multitude, "Repent, and each one of you be baptized in the name of Jesus Christ for the remission of sins, and you will receive the gift of the Holy Spirit. For the promise is for you and your children and for all who are far off, as many as the Lord our God will call to Himself."

And with many other words he solemnly testified and kept on exhorting them, saying, "Be saved from this perverse generation!"

And so then, those who had received his word were baptized; and that day were added about three thousand souls.

¤ And there is salvation in no one else; for there is no other name under heaven that has been given among men by which we must be saved.

Matthew 3:13-17, Mark 16:15, 16, Acts 2:38-41, Acts 4:12

June 9th / December 9th

And the Spirit said to Philip, "Go up and join his chariot."

Philip ran up to the chariot and heard the Ethiopian eunuch reading Isaiah the prophet. Philip then said to him, "Do you understand what you are reading?"

And the man replied, "Well, how can I, unless someone guides me?" He then invited Philip to come up and sit with him. Now the passage of Scripture which he was reading was this:

"He was led as a sheep to the slaughter; and as a lamb before its shearer is silent, so He does not open His mouth. In humiliation His judgment was taken away; who will describe His family origin? For His life is removed from the earth."

The man then questioned Philip, "Please tell me, of whom does the prophet say this?"

Then Philip opened his mouth, and beginning from that Scripture he preached Jesus to him. And as they traveled along the road they came to some water, and the man said,

"Look! Here is water! What prevents me from being baptized?"

And Philip said, "If you believe with all of your heart, you may."

And the man answered him, "I believe that Jesus Christ is the Son of God."

He then ordered the chariot to stop; and they both went down into the water, and Philip baptized him. When they came up out of the water, the Spirit of the Lord snatched Philip away; and the man no longer saw him, but went on his way rejoicing.

¤ Go and make disciples of all nations, baptizing them in the name of the Father and the Son and the Holy Ghost.

Acts 8:29-39, Matthew 28:19

194

June 10th / December 10th

Saul breathed threats and murder against the disciples of the Lord.

He was approaching Damascus, and suddenly a light from heaven flashed around him; and he fell to the ground and heard a voice saying to him, "Saul, Saul, why are you persecuting Me?" And Saul said, "Who are You, Lord?"

And the voice answered, "I am Jesus whom your are persecuting, but get up and enter the city, and it will be told you what you must do."

The men who traveled with Saul stood speechless, hearing the voice but seeing no one. Saul got up from the ground, and though his eyes were open, he could see nothing; and leading him by the hand, they brought him into Damascus. And he was three days without sight, and neither ate nor drank...

A disciple named Ananias entered the house, and after laying his hands on him, said, "Brother Saul, the Lord Jesus, who appeared to you on the road by which you were coming, has sent me so that you may regain your sight and be filled with the Holy Spirit."

And immediately there fell from his eyes something like scales, and he regained his sight, and he got up and was baptized; and he took food and was strengthened. Now for several days he was with the disciples who were at Damascus, and immediately he began to proclaim Jesus in the synagogues, saying, "He is the Son of God."

¤ Now why do you delay? Get up and be baptized, and wash away your sins, calling on His name.

Acts 9:1, 3-9, 17-20, Acts 22:16

June 11ᵗʰ / December 11ᵗʰ

*And suddenly there came a great
earthquake...*

The foundations of the prison house were shaken, and immediately all the doors were opened and everyone's chains unfastened. When the jailer awoke and saw the prison doors opened, he drew his sword and was about to kill himself, supposing that the prisoners had escaped.

But Paul cried out with a loud voice, saying, "Do not harm yourself, for we are all here!"

So the jailer called for lights and rushed in, and trembling with fear he fell down before Paul and Silas. Then after he had brought them out, he said, "Sirs, what must I do to be saved?"

And they said, "Believe in the Lord Jesus Christ, and you will be saved, you and your household." And Paul and Silas spoke the word to the man together with all those who were in his house. And the man took them that very hour of the night and washed their wounds, and immediately he was baptized, the man and all of his household. And he brought Paul and Silas into his house and set food before them, and rejoiced greatly, having believed in God with his whole household.

¤ A woman named Lydia, from the city of Thyatira, a seller of purple fabrics, a worshiper of God, was listening; and the Lord opened her heart to respond to the things spoken by Paul. And when she and her household had been baptized, she urged Paul and his companions, saying, "If you have judged me to be faithful to the Lord, come into my house and stay." And she prevailed upon them.

¤ Whoever believes and is baptized will be saved.

Acts 16:26-34, Acts 16:14, 15, Mark 16:16

196

June 12th
December 12th

Make me to know Your ways, O Lord; teach me Your paths. Lead me in Your truth and teach me, for You are the God of my salvation.

¤ Paul took the road through the interior and arrived at Ephesus. There he found some disciples and asked them, "Did you receive the Holy Spirit when you believed?"

They answered, "No, we have not so much as heard whether there is a Holy Spirit."

So Paul asked, "Into what then were you baptized?"

"Into John's baptism," they replied.

Paul then said, "John's baptism was a baptism of repentance. He told the people to believe in the One coming after him, that is, in Jesus."

Upon hearing this, the men were baptized into the name of the Lord Jesus. ¤ And there is salvation in no one else; for there is no other name under heaven that has been given among men by which we must be saved.

¤ Paul went to the house of Titius Justus, a worshiper of God, whose house was next to the synagogue. Then Crispus also, the synagogue ruler, and his entire household believed in the Lord; and many of the Corinthians, who heard him, believed and were baptized.

¤ Baptism now saves you also—not the removal of the filth of the flesh (the sinful nature), but the answer of a good conscience toward God through the resurrection of Jesus Christ.

Psalm 25:4, 5, Acts 19:1-5, Acts 4:12, Acts 18:7, 8, 1st Peter 3:21

197

June 13ᵗʰ / December 13ᵗʰ

He who goes out weeping carrying seed to sow, will return with songs of joy carrying sheaves with him.

¤ Sow for yourselves righteousness, reap the fruit of unfailing love, and break up your unploughed ground; for it is time to seek the Lord, until He comes and showers righteousness upon you.

¤ Praise be the God and Father of our Lord Jesus Christ! In His great mercy He has given us new birth into a living hope through the resurrection of Jesus Christ from the dead, and into an inheritance that can never perish, spoil or fade—kept in heaven for you, who through faith are shielded by God's power until the coming of the salvation that is ready to be revealed in the last time.

In this you greatly rejoice, though now for a little while you may have had to suffer grief in all kinds of trials. These have come so that your faith—of greater worth than gold, which perishes even though refined by fire—may be proved genuine and may result in praise, glory and honor when Jesus Christ is revealed.

Though you have not seen Him, you love Him; and believe in Him and are filled with an inexpressible and glorious joy, for you are receiving the goal of your faith, the salvation of your souls... Even angels long to look into these things. ¤ Let us not become weary in doing good, for at the proper time we will reap a harvest of blessing if we do not get discouraged and give up. Therefore, as we have opportunity, let us do good to all people, especially to those who belong to the family of believers.

Psalm 126:6, Hosea 10:12, 1ˢᵗ Peter 1:3-9, 12, Galatians 6:9, 10

June 14th / December 14th

For the sake of Your name, O Lord, forgive my iniquity, though it is great.

Who, then is the man/woman that fears the Lord? He will instruct them in the way chosen for them. They will spend their days in prosperity, and their descendants will inherit the land.

¤ By day the Lord went ahead of them in a pillar of cloud to guide them on their way, and by night in a pillar of fire to give them light, so that they could travel by day or night. Neither the pillar of cloud by day nor the pillar of fire by night left its place in front of the people.

¤ Your word is a lamp to my feet and a light to my path... I keep Your precepts and Your testimonies, for all my ways are before You. ¤ Whether I turn to the right or to the left, my ears will hear a voice behind me, saying, "This is the way; walk in it." ¤ All the paths of the Lord are mercy and truth, to such as keep His covenant and His testimonies.

¤ I know, O Lord, that a man's/woman's life is not their own; it is not for us to direct our steps. Correct me Lord, but only with justice—not in Your anger, lest You reduce me to nothing.

¤ "I will instruct you and teach you in the way you should go," says the Lord. "I will counsel you and watch over you. Do not be like the horse or the mule, which have no understanding but must be controlled by bit and bridle, or they will not come to you." Many are the woes of the wicked, but the Lord's unfailing love surrounds those who trust in Him.

Psalm 25:11-13, Exodus 13:21, 22, Psalm 119:105, 168, Isaiah 30:21, Psalm 25:10, Jeremiah 10:23, 24, Psalm 32:8-10

June 15th / December 15th

When you lie down, you will not be afraid.

Yes, you will lie down and your sleep will be sweet. Do not be afraid of sudden terror, nor trouble from the wicked when it comes; for the Lord will be your confidence, and will keep your foot from being caught.

¤ A great windstorm arose, and the waves beat into the boat, so that it was nearly swamped. Jesus was in the stern, sleeping on a cushion. The disciples woke Him up and said to Him, "Teacher, do you not care if we drown?"

Then Jesus arose and rebuked the wind, and said to the sea, "Peace—be still!" And the wind ceased and there was a great calm. But He said to them, "Why are you so fearful? How is it that you have no faith?" And they feared exceedingly, and said to one another, "Who can this be, that even the wind and the sea obey Him!"

¤ Do not be anxious about anything, but in everything, by prayer and petition, with thanksgiving, present your requests to God. And the peace of God, which transcends all understanding, will guard your hearts and your minds as your trust in Christ Jesus. ¤ I love the Lord because He has heard my voice and my supplications, because He has inclined His ear to me. Therefore I will call upon Him as long as I live... Gracious is the Lord and righteous; Yes our God is merciful. The Lord preserves the simple; I was brought low and He saved me; Return to your rest, O my soul, for the Lord has dealt bountifully with you.

Proverbs 3:24-26, Mark 4:37-41, Philippians 4:6, 7,
Psalm 116:1, 2, 5-7

June 16th / December 16th

The lamp of the Lord searches the spirit of a man; it searches out his inmost being.

¤ He will not always accuse, nor will He harbor His anger forever; He does not treat us as our sins deserve, nor repay us according to our iniquities. For as high as the heavens are above the earth, so great is His love for those who fear Him; as far as the east is from the west, so far He has removed our transgressions from us. As a father has compassion on his children, so the Lord has compassion on those who fear Him; for He knows how we are formed; He remembers that we are but dust.

As for man his days are like grass, he flourishes like a flower of the field; the wind blows over it and it is gone, and its place remembers it no more. But from everlasting to everlasting the Lord's love is with those who fear Him, and His righteousness with their children's children—with those who keep His covenant and remember to obey His precepts.

¤ He who heeds discipline shows the way to life, but whoever ignores correction leads others astray. He who conceals his hatred has lying lips, and whoever spreads slander is a fool. When words are many, sin is not absent, but he who holds his tongue is wise. The tongue of the righteous is as choice sliver, but the heart of the wicked is of little value. The lips of the righteous nourish many, but fools die for lack of judgment.

¤ Teach me Your way, O Lord; I will walk in Your truth.

Proverbs 20:27, Psalm 103:9-18, Proverbs 10:17-21, Psalm 86:11

June 17th / December 17th

Woe to those who carry out plans that are not Mine.

They form an alliance, but not by My Spirit, heaping sin upon sin... These are rebellious people, deceitful children, children unwilling to listen to the Lord's instruction. The say to the seers, "See no more visions!" and to the prophets, "Give us no more visions of what is right! Tell us pleasant things, prophesy illusions. Leave this way, get off this path, and stop confronting us with the Holy one of Israel!"

¤ Therefore this is what the Lord Almighty says: "I will refine and test them, for what else can I do because of the sin of My people? Their tongue is a deadly arrow; it speaks with deceit. With his mouth each speaks cordially to his neighbor, but in his heart he sets a trap for him. Should I not punish them for this: Should I not avenge Myself on a people such as this?"

¤ I remember my affliction and my wandering; the bitterness and the gall. I well remember them, and my soul is downcast within me. Yet, I call this to mind and therefore I have hope: Because of the Lord's great love we are not consumed, for His compassion's never fail. His mercy is new every morning; great is His faithfulness. I say to myself, "The Lord is my portion; therefore I will wait for Him."

The Lord is good to those whose hope is in Him, to the one who seeks Him; It is good to wait quietly for the salvation of the Lord... Let one bury their face into the dust of the earth—there may yet be hope.

Isaiah 30:1, 9-11, Jeremiah 9:7-9, Lamentations 3:19-26, 29

June 18ᵗʰ / December 18ᵗʰ

Do not boast about tomorrow, for you do not know what a day may bring forth.

¤ Do not receive God's grace in vain. For He says, "In the time of favor I heard you, and in the day of salvation I helped you." I tell you now is the time of God's favor, now is the day of salvation.

¤ A little while longer the light is with you. Walk while you have the light, lest darkness overtake you. He/she who walks in darkness does not know where they are going. While you have the light, believe in the light, that you may become sons and daughters of light.

¤ Whatever your hand finds to do, do it with all your might, for in the grave, where you are going, there is neither working nor planning, nor knowledge, nor wisdom. ¤ A man said to his soul, "I have many goods laid up for many years; take your ease; eat, drink, and be merry."

But God said to him, "Fool! This night your very soul will be required of you. Whose then will those things be that you have stored up for yourself? This is how it will be with anyone who stores up things for themselves but is not rich toward God."

¤ You are a mist that appears for a little while and then vanishes away. Instead, you ought to say, "If it is the Lord's will, we will live and do this or that." But you instead boast in your arrogance. All such boasting is evil. ¤ To be carnally minded is death, but to be spiritually minded is life and peace.

Proverbs 27:1, 2ⁿᵈ Corinthians 6:1, 2, John 12:35, 36,
Ecclesiastes 9:10, Luke 12:19-21, Romans 8:6

June 19th / December 19th

I sought Him, but I did not find Him.

¤ Return to the Lord your God. Your sins have been your downfall. Take words with you and return to the Lord. Say to Him, "Forgive all my sins and receive me graciously, that I may offer the fruit of my lips." ...Who is wise? He/she will realize these things. Who is discerning? He/she will understand them.

¤ Let no one say when they are tempted, "I am tempted by God," for God cannot be tempted by evil, nor does He Himself tempt anyone. But each person is tempted when they are drawn away by their own desires and enticed. Then, after desire has conceived, it gives birth to sin, and sin, when it is full grown, gives birth to death. Don't be deceived. Every good gift and every perfect gift is from above, and comes down from the Father of lights, with whom there is no variation nor shadow of turning.

¤ Wait on the Lord; be of good courage, and He shall strengthen your heart. ¤ And will God not bring about justice for His chosen ones, who cry out to Him day and night? Will He keep putting them off? I tell you, He will see that they get justice, and quickly. However, when the Son of Man comes, will He find faith on the earth?

¤ Hear my cry, O God; attend to my prayer. From the end of the earth I will cry to You, when my heart is overwhelmed. Lead me to the Rock that is higher than I. For You have been a shelter for me; a strong tower from the enemy.

Song 3:2, Hosea 14:1, 2, 9, James 1:13-17, Psalm 27:14, Luke 18:7, 8, Psalm 61:1-3

June 20th / December 20th

Remember, the Lord forgave you, so
you must forgive others.

¤ And Jesus said, "Two men owed money to a certain moneylender. One owed him five hundred denarii, and the other fifty. Neither one of them had the money to pay him back, and so he canceled the debts of both men. Now which of them will love him more?"

Simon replied, "I suppose the one who had the bigger debt canceled."

"You have judged correctly," Jesus said. ¤ "If you forgive those who sin against you, your heavenly Father will also forgive you. But if you do not forgive others of their sins, your Father will not forgive you of your sins."

¤ Then Peter came to Jesus and asked, "Lord, how many times shall I forgive my brother when he sins against me. Up to seven times?"

Jesus said to him, "I do not say to you, up to seven times, but up to seventy times seven." ¤ The Lord is kind to the unthankful and evil. Therefore, be merciful, just as your Father also is merciful. Judge not, and you shall not be judged, Condemn not, and you shall not be condemned. Forgive, and you will be forgiven.

¤ To the Lord our God belong mercy and forgiveness, though we have rebelled against Him. We have not obeyed the voice of the Lord our God, to walk in His laws, which He has set before us.

Colossians 3;13, Luke 7:41-43, Matthew 6:14, 15, Matthew 18:21, 22,
Luke 6:35-37, Daniel 9:9, 10

June 21st / December 21st

He Himself bore our sins.

He bore them in His own body on the tree, that we, having died to sins, might live for righteousness—by His wounds you have been healed. For you were like sheep going astray, but now have returned to the Shepherd and Overseer of your souls.

¤ You were taught, with regard to your former way of life, to put off your old self, which is corrupted by its evil desires, and to be made new in the attitude of your minds, and put on the new self, created to be like God in true righteousness and holiness. Therefore each of you must put off falsehood and speak truthfully with his neighbor, for we are all members of one body... Be kind and compassionate to one another, forgiving each other, just as in Christ God forgave you.

¤ We died to sin; how can we live in it any longer? Do you not know that those of us who were baptized into Christ Jesus were baptized into his death? We were therefore buried with Him through baptism into death, in order that, just as Christ was raised from the dead by the glory of the Father, we too may walk in newness of life.

For if we have been united with Him in the likeness of His death, we will certainly also be in the likeness of His resurrection; knowing this; that our old man was crucified with Him, that the body of sin might be done away with, and that we should no longer be slaves of sin. For he who has died has been freed from sin. Now if we died with Christ, we believe that we shall also live with Him.

¤ But the natural man does not accept the things of the Spirit of God... and he cannot understand them, because these things are spiritually discerned.

1ˢᵗ Peter 2:24, 25, Ephesians 4:22-25, 32, Romans 6:2-8,
1ˢᵗ Corinthians 2:14

207

June 22nd / December 22nd

At daybreak Jesus went out to a solitary place.

¤ Simon and his companions went to look for Him, and when they found Him, they exclaimed: "Everyone is looking for You!"

Jesus then replied, "Let us go somewhere else—to the nearby villages—so that I can teach there also. This is why I have come." So he traveled throughout Galilee, teaching in their synagogues and driving out demons.

¤ Give thanks to the Lord, for He is good, His love endures forever; let the redeemed of the Lord say this—those He redeemed from the hand of the foe, those He gathered from the lands, from east and west, from north and south. Some wandered in desert wastelands, finding no way to a city where they could settle. They were hungry and thirsty, and their lives ebbed away. Then they cried out to the Lord in their trouble, and He delivered them from their distress.

¤ Jesus declared, "I am the bread of life. He/she who comes to Me will never go hungry, and those who believe in Me will never be thirsty. But as I told you, you have seen Me and still you do not believe. All those whom the Father gives Me will come to Me, and whomever comes to Me I will never drive away. For I have come down from heaven not to do My will, but to do the will of Him who sent me.

"And this is the will of Him who sent Me; that I shall lose none of those that He has given Me, but raise them up at the last day. For My Father's will is that everyone who looks to the Son, and believes in Him, shall have eternal life, and I will raise them up at the last day."

Luke 4:42, Mark 1:36-39, Psalm 107:1-6, John 6:35-40

June 23rd / December 23rd

"Sanctify them by Your truth. Your word is truth...

"I do not ask on behalf of these alone, but also for those who will believe in Me through their word; that they all may be one, as You, Father, are in Me, and I in You; that they also may be one in Us, that the world may believe that You have sent Me....

"Father, I desire that they also whom You have given Me may be with Me where I am, that they may behold My glory which You have given Me; for You loved Me before the foundation of the world."

¤ Now therefore, fear the Lord, serve Him in sincerity and in truth, and put away the gods which your fathers served on the other side of the River and in Egypt. Serve the Lord! And if it seems evil to you to serve the Lord, then choose for yourselves this day whom you will serve, whether the gods which your fathers served that were on the other side of the River, or the gods of the Amorites, in whose land you dwell. But as for me and my house, we will serve the Lord.

¤ He appointed the moon for seasons; the sun knows its going down. You make the darkness, and it is night, in which the beasts of the forest creep about. The young lions roar after their prey, and seek their food from God. When the sun rises they gather together and lie down in their dens. Man goes out to his work and to his labor until the evening.

O Lord, how manifold are Your works! In wisdom you have made them all. The earth is full of your possessions... May sinners be consumed from the earth, and the wicked be no more.

John 17:17, 20, 21, 24, Joshua 24:14, 15, Psalm 104:19-24, 35

June 24th / December 24th

"A certain man planted a vineyard, leased it to vine-dressers, and went into a far country for a long time.

"Now at vintage time he sent a servant to the vine-dressers, that they might give him some of the fruit of the vineyard. But the vine-dressers beat him and sent him away empty handed.

"Again he sent another servant; and they beat him also, treated him shamefully, and sent him away empty handed. And so he sent a third, and they wounded him also and cast him out.

"Then the owner of the vineyard said, 'What shall I do? I will send my beloved son. Perhaps they will respect him when they see him.'

"But when the vine-dressers saw him, they reasoned among themselves, saying, 'This is the heir. Come, let us kill him, that the inheritance may be ours.' So they cast him out of the vineyard and killed him. Therefore, what will the owner of the vineyard do to them? He will come and destroy the vine-dressers and give the vineyard to others."

When the chief priests and scribes heard this story they said, "Certainly not!"

But Jesus looked at them and said, "What then is this that is written: 'The stone which the builders rejected has become the chief cornerstone'? Whoever falls on that stone will be broken; but on whomever it falls, it will grind him to powder."

And the chief priests and the scribes that very hour sought to lay hands on Him, but they feared the people—for they knew that He had spoken this parable against them.

Luke 20:9-19

June 25th / December 25th

*As they led Him away, they seized
Simon from Cyrene, who was on his
way in from the country, and on him
they laid the cross and made him carry
it behind Jesus.*

A great multitude of the people followed Him, including women who also mourned and lamented Him. But Jesus, turning to them, said, "Daughters of Jerusalem, do not weep for Me, but weep for yourselves and for your children. For indeed the days are coming in which they will say, 'Blessed are the barren, wombs that never bore, and breasts which never nursed!' Then they will begin to say to the mountains, 'Fall on us!' and to the hills, 'Cover us!' For if they do these things in the green wood, what will be done in the dry?"

There were also two others, criminals, led with Him to be put to death. And when they had come to the place called Calvary, there they crucified Him, and the criminals, one on the right hand and the other on the left.

Then Jesus said, "Father, forgive them, for they do not know what they do."

...One of the criminals then said to Jesus, "Lord, remember me when You come into Your kingdom."

And Jesus said to him, "Assuredly, I say to you, today you will be with Me in paradise."

...And when Jesus had cried out with a loud voice, He said, "Father, into Your hands I commit My spirit."

Having said this, He breathed His last. When a centurion saw what had happened, he glorified God, saying, "Certainly this was a righteous man!"

Luke 23:26-34, 42, 43, 46, 47

211

June 26ᵗʰ / December 26ᵗʰ

Joseph, a counsel member, took down the body of Jesus, wrapped it in linen, and laid it in a tomb that was hewn out of the rock, where no one had ever lain before.

¤ After the Sabbath, at dawn on the first day of the week, Mary Magdalene and the other Mary went to look at the tomb. There was a violent earthquake, for an angel of the Lord came down from heaven and, going to the tomb, rolled back the stone and sat upon it. His appearance was like lightning, and his clothes were as white as snow. The guards were so afraid of him that they shook and became like dead men.

Then the angel said to the women, "Do not be afraid, for I know that you are looking for Jesus, who was crucified. He is not here; He has risen, just as He said. Come and see the place where He lay. Then go quickly and tell His disciples: 'He has risen from the dead and is going on ahead of you into Galilee. There you will see Him.' Now I have told you."

So the women hurried away from the tomb, afraid yet filled with joy, and ran to tell His disciples. Suddenly Jesus met them.

"Rejoice!" He said.

The women came to Him, clasped His feet and worshiped Him. Jesus then said to them, "Do not be afraid, but go and tell My brothers to go to Galilee; there they will see Me."

...Then Jesus came to them and said, "All authority has been given to Me in heaven and on earth. Go therefore and make disciples of all nations, baptizing them in the name of the Father and of the Son and of the Holy Spirit. Teach them to observe all things that I have commanded you. And surely I am with you always, even to the very end of the age."

Luke 23:50-53, Matthew 28:1-10, 18-20

212

June 27th / December 27th

There is no condemnation for those who are in Christ Jesus, who do not walk according to the flesh, but according to the Spirit.

For the law of the Spirit of life in Christ Jesus has set us free from the law of sin and death. For what the law was powerless to do, in that it was weakened by the sinful nature, God did by sending His own Son in the likeness of sinful man to be a sin offering. And so, He condemned sin in sinful man, in order that the righteous requirements of the law might be fully met in us, who do not live according to our sinful nature, but according to the Spirit.

Those who live according to the sinful nature have their minds set on what that nature desires; but those who live in accordance with the Spirit have their minds set on what the Spirit desires. For to be carnally minded is death, but to be spiritually minded is life and peace. Because the carnal mind is hostile toward God, it does not submit itself to the law of God, nor can it do so. Those who are controlled by the sinful nature cannot please God.

You, however, are controlled not by the sinful nature, but by the Spirit, if the Spirit of God lives in you. And if anyone does not have the Spirit of Christ, he/she does not belong to Christ. But if Christ is in you, your body is dead because of sin, yet your spirit is alive because of righteousness. And if the Spirit of Him who raised Jesus from the dead is living in you, He who raised Christ from the dead will also give life to your mortal bodies through the Spirit, who lives in you.

Romans 8:1-11

June 28th / December 28th

We have an obligation—but it is not to our sinful nature; to live according to it.

For if you live according to your sinful nature, you will die. But if by the Spirit you put to death the misdeeds of the body, you will live, because those who are led by the Spirit of God are the sons/daughters of God. For you did not receive the spirit of bondage that makes you a slave again to fear, but you received the Spirit of adoption... The Spirit Himself bears witness with our spirit that we are children of God.

Now if we are children, then we are heirs—heirs of God and co-heirs with Christ, if indeed we share in His sufferings in order that we may also share in His glory. I consider that our present sufferings are not worth comparing with the glory that shall be revealed in us... And He who searches our hearts knows the mind of the Spirit, because the Spirit intercedes for the saints in accordance with God's will.

¤ No eye has seen, nor ear has heard, no mind has conceived what God has prepared for those who love Him. But God has revealed it to us by His Spirit. The Spirit searches all things, even the deep things of God.

¤ You are all children of God through faith in Christ Jesus, for all of you who were baptized into Christ have clothed yourself with Christ. There is neither Jew nor Greek, slave nor free, male nor female, for you are all one in Christ Jesus. ¤ You were once darkness, but now you are light in the Lord. Walk as children of light.

Romans 8:12-18, 27, 1st Corinthians 2:9, 10, Galatians 3:26-28, Ephesians 5:8

June 29th / December 29th

In the last days perilous times will come.

For men will be lovers of themselves, lovers of money, boastful, proud, abusive, disobedient to their parents, ungrateful, unholy, without love, unforgiving, slanderous, without self-control, brutal, not lovers of the good, treacherous, rash, conceited, lovers of pleasure rather than lovers of God—having a form of godliness but denying its power. Have nothing to do with them...

All Scripture is given by the inspiration of God, and is useful for teaching, rebuking, correcting and training in what is right, so that the followers of God may be thoroughly equipped for every good work.

¤ See to it that you do not refuse Him who speaks. For if they did not escape who refused Him who spoke on the earth, how much less will we, if we turn away from Him who warns us from heaven? At that time His voice shook the earth, but now He has promised, "Once more I will shake not only the earth, but also the heavens."

The words "once more" indicate the removing of what can be shaken—that is, created things—so that what cannot be shaken may remain. Therefore, since we have received a kingdom that cannot be shaken, let us be thankful, and so worship God acceptably with reverence and awe, for our "God is a consuming fire."

2nd Timothy 3:1-5, 16, 17, Hebrews 12:25-29

215

June 30th / December 30th

Resist the devil, and he will flee from you.

¤ Each of you must put off falsehood and speak truthfully to your neighbor, for we are all members of one body. In your anger do not sin. Do not let the sun go down while you are still angry, and do not give the devil a foothold. Those who have been stealing must steal no longer, but must work, doing something useful with their own hands, that they may have something to share with those in need.

Do not let any unwholesome talk come out of your mouths, but only what is helpful for building others up according to their needs; that it may benefit those who listen. And do not grieve the Holy Spirit of God, with whom you were sealed for the day of redemption. Get rid of all bitterness, rage and anger, brawling and slander, along with every form of malice. Be kind and compassionate to one another, forgiving each other, just as in Christ God forgave you.

¤ Do you not know? Have you not heard? The Lord is the everlasting God, the Creator of the ends of the earth. He will not grow tired or weary, and increases the strength of the weak. Even youths grow tired and weary, and young men stumble and fall; but those who hope in the Lord will renew their strength. They will soar on wings like eagles; they will run and not grow weary, they will walk and not be faint.

¤ To you who fear My name, the Sun of righteousness shall arise with healing in its wings. ¤ To shine on those living in darkness and in the shadow of death.

James 4:7, Ephesians 4:25-32, Isaiah 40:28-31, Luke 1:79

December 31ˢᵗ

*One thing God has spoken, two
things I have heard...*

That You, O God, are strong,
and that You, O Lord, are loving. Surely You will reward each
person according to what he/she has done.

¤ The Lord gave the word; great was the company of those
who proclaimed it... Sing to God, you kingdoms of the earth; O
sing praises to the Lord. To Him who rides on the heaven of
heavens, which were of old! Indeed He sends out His voice, a
mighty voice. Ascribe strength to God; His excellence is over all
of His people, and His strength is in the clouds. O God, You are
more awesome than Your holy places. Our God is He who gives
strength and power to His people.

¤ In You, O Lord, I put my trust; let me never be put to
shame. Deliver me in Your righteousness, and cause me to
escape. Incline Your ear to me, and save me. Be my strong
refuge, to which I may resort continually; You have given the
commandment to save me, for You are my rock and my fortress.

Deliver me, O my God, out of the hand of the wicked, out of
the hand of unrighteous and cruel men. For You are my hope, O
Lord God; You are my trust from my youth. By You I have been
upheld from birth; You are He who took me out of my mother's
womb. My praise shall be continually of You...

From my youth, O God, You have taught me, and to this
day I declare Your wondrous works. Now also when I am old
and gray headed, do not forsake me, O God, until I declare Your
strength to this generation, Your power to everyone who is to
come... My tongue shall speak of Your righteousness all the day
long.

Psalm 62:11, 12, Psalm 68:11, 32-35, Psalm 71:1-6, 17, 18, 24

And out of the ground the Lord God made every tree grow that is pleasant to the sight and good for food. The tree of life was also in the midst of the garden, and the tree of the knowledge of good and evil.

Genesis 2:9

References and Notes

1...(pg 14) 'She'—The Spirit of Wisdom is *female* in nature. That is most interesting.

2...(pg 36) The Ark—*Note*: There are those who do not believe that the Ark could have contained all the pairs of animals and birds that God chose to bring aboard it. There's evidently some misunderstanding here; the Ark had a capacity of nearly 3,600,000 cubic feet. In reality, nearly 1000 railroad boxcars could fit into a ship of this size—more than enough room for the chosen species and ample room to spare for food.

3...(pg 66) DNA (deoxyribonucleic acid) contains uniquely coded information that determines what you look like, much of your personality, and how every cell in your body is to function throughout your lifetime. If the DNA (46 segments; 23 from your mother and 23 from your father) in *one* of your cells were uncoiled, connected and stretched out, it would be about 7 feet long. However, if all of this very 'densely coded information' from *one* cell of *one* person were written in books, it would fill a library of about 4000 books.

You have duplicate copies of this DNA in each of the 100,000,000,000,000 (one hundred trillion) cells in your body. If the coded DNA information in *your body* were placed end to end, it would stretch from the earth to the moon 500,000 times. However, if one set of DNA (one cell's worth) from every person who ever lived were placed in a pile, it would weigh less than an aspirin!

All of this unfathomable construction can be translated *fearfully and wonderfully made.*

4...(pg 81, pg 101) Psalm 118:8 is the very center of the Bible. Psalm 117, before Psalm 118 is the shortest chapter in the Bible. Psalm 119, before Psalm 118 is the longest chapter in the Bible. The Bible has 594 chapters before Psalm 118 and 594 Chapters after Psalm 118. If you add up all the chapters except Psalm 118, you get a total of 1188 chapters. 1188—Psalm 118 verse 8, is the middle verse of the entire Bible. Is this central verse not also the central theme of the entire Bible? This is not a coincidence. God is in complete control.

5...(pg 143) At the tower of Babel (Genesis 11:1-9), God confused the human language, which at that time (approximately 200 years after the flood) everyone spoke the same language. After the language division came about the people were scattered all over the face of the earth.

Note: Languages are related, as are human genes. One of thousands of examples is the word for "from" or "of". It exists in French (*de*), Italian (*di*), Spanish (*de*), Portuguese (*de*), and Romanian (*de*). These languages, now spoken generally in southwestern Europe, are twigs on a tree branch called the Romance languages (Romance meaning *Rome*).

This branch joins a larger branch that includes all

languages derived primarily from Latin. They merge with other large branches, such as the Germanic branch that includes English, into a family called the Indo-European languages. When these and other languages are traced back in time, they converge near the Mountains of Ararat.

The name Babel gives us our word "to babble," meaning, "to utter meaningless sounds." Most scholars place Babel's location somewhere between today's Tigris and Euphrates Rivers, near the sight of ancient Babylon and the mountains of Ararat, where Noah's Ark landed (Genesis 8:4).

6...(page 145) Psalm 139:14, 'Fearfully and Wonderfully made.' See DNA information at References and Notes # **3**.

Reader's Notes:

75097556R00134

Made in the USA
Columbia, SC
15 August 2017